505
RADIO
QUESTIONS
YOUR FRIENDS
CAN'T ANSWER

Other books in this series:

505 Baseball Questions Your Friends Can't Answer
(updated and revised)
John Kingston
505 Football Questions Your Friends Can't Answer
(updated and revised)
Harold Rosenthal
505 Hockey Questions Your Friends Can't Answer
Frank Polnaszek
505 Basketball Questions Your Friends Can't Answer
Sol Barzman
505 Boxing Questions Your Friends Can't Answer
Bert Sugar and John Grasso
and also:
505 Rock 'n' Roll Questions Your Friends Can't Answer
Nicholas and Elizabeth Schaffner
505 Movie Questions Your Friends Can't Answer
Louis Phillips
505 Theatre Questions Your Friends Can't Answer
John Beaufort
505 Wine Questions Your Friends Can't Answer
Carole Collier
505 Television Questions Your Friends Can't Answer
Harry Castleman and Walter J.Podrazik

Other books by Castleman and Podrazik

All Together Now
The Beatles Again
The End of the Beatles
The TV Schedule Book
Watching TV

505 RADIO QUESTIONS

YOUR FRIENDS CAN'T ANSWER

HARRY CASTLEMAN AND WALTER J. PODRAZIK

WALKER AND COMPANY
NEW YORK

First published in the United States of America
in 1983 by the Walker Publishing Company, Inc.

Published simultaneously in Canada by John Wiley & Sons
Canada, Limited, Rexdale, Ontario.

ISBN: 0-8027-7211-0

Library of Congress Catalog Card Number: 83-42742

Printed in the United States of America

10 9 8 7 6 5 4 3 2 1

Library of Congress Cataloging in Publication Data
Castleman, Harry
  505 radio questions your friends can't answer.

  1. Radio broadcasting—United States—Miscellanea.
I. Podrazik, Walter J. II. Title. III. Title:
Five hundred five radio questions your friends can't
answer. IV. Title: Five hundred five radio
questions your friends can't answer.
PN991.3.U6C37   1983   791.44   83-42742
ISBN 0-8027-7211-0 (pbk.)

Contents

Foreword

Radio is special.

From the pioneer broadcasts at the turn of the century to the latest satellite-fed signals, radio has brought a touch of magic into our lives. Unencumbered by visuals, radio appeals directly to our imaginations, letting us set the stage for great drama, comedy, adventure, news coverage, sports contests, and music. More important, radio is a warm, personal medium that has served as our special companion for several generations.

This book, then, is an affectionate visit with an old friend.

To make this visit as much fun as possible, we've downplayed isolated, unconnected facts in our trivia questions in favor of more anecdotal items. That way, even if you miss a few, there are always the stories themselves to serve as entertaining memory-joggers. So choose your favorite era and step back with us into a very special world.

First, though, we'd like to thank: friends Ed Mann, John O'Leary, Tom Schultheiss, and Mark Nelson for resource information along the way; Joe Federici, Laura Janis, and Barbara Brown for first draft comments and criticism; and PJ Haduch and Nicholas Schaffner for the initial nudge. We'd also like to heartily recommend a visit to the Museum of Broadcasting in New York City for firsthand exposure to classic moments in radio history, and two excellent reference books for more detailed background information: *Don't Touch That Dial* by J. Fred MacDonald and *Tune in Yesterday* by John Dunning.

Above all, we'd like to thank the many radio enthusiasts who collected and preserved the golden moments from the 1930s and 1940s. We grew up with and loved rock 'n' roll radio during the 1950s and

1960s, but, thanks to their efforts, we also heard and enjoyed the offerings from that previous era.

And now, once again, forward—into the past.

Harry Castleman and Wally Podrazik

SWITCH ON/
TUNE IN

Switch On/
Tune In

1. Listeners across the country panicked on the night of October 30, 1938, convinced that Martians (or worse!) had landed. What was really going on?

2. What power did the Shadow possess?

3. What radio series was so popular in the early 1930s that movie houses promised to stop their films from 7:00 to 7:15 P.M. so that the radio show could be piped in?

4. On March 12, 1933, President Franklin Roosevelt instituted a special series of national radio broadcasts. What were they called?

5. What happened when Fibber McGee opened his closet door?

6. Where did Titus Moody, Mrs. Nussbaum, and Senator Claghorn all live?

7. What western adventure series led to the formation of the Mutual radio network in the early 1930s?

8. Who was the "all-American boy" from Hudson High School?

9. What sponsor offered such premiums as secret decoders and shake-up mugs on *Little Orphan Annie* in the 1930s and on *Captain Midnight* in the 1940s?

10. The rapid-fire chant of a tobacco auctioneer was part of the familiar opening of *Your Hit Parade*. Name the sponsor.

11. Johnny Roventini, a 4-foot-tall bellhop, uttered the most famous "page" in radio history. What was it?

12. In 1937 the *Major Bowes Original Amateur Hour* presented a young singing group that included a performer who would later become an entertainment superstar. Who was he?

13. The theatrical film *The Big Broadcast of 1938* featured Bob Hope singing what would become his theme song. What was it?

14. What syndicated Christmas serial presented the adventures of Judy and Jimmy Barton and their search for the Silver Star?

15. Who was radio's biggest workaholic (and CBS's biggest money-maker) in the 1940s, holding down daytime, prime time, and weekend slots?

16. Who was the creator, writer, producer, director, and star of *The Goldbergs*?

17. Allen Funt first presented people "caught in the act of being themselves" on what late-1940s series?

18. What comedy-program opening caught listeners with the distinctive warning: "Uh-uh-uhh. Don't touch that dial"?

19. Name the public-affairs show set up on Mutual in 1945 as a live, unrehearsed "press conference of the air," featuring a major newsmaker taking questions from a panel of journalists.

20. How did the studio audience complete this introduction, used on a popular quiz show: "Here he is, the one, the only—"?

21. What question did host Jack Bailey use to open every broadcast of *Queen for a Day*?

22. What comedy series role endeared Eve Arden to teachers throughout the country?

23. What police series opened with the chilling theme "Dum-de-dum-dum" and the assurance that the story to follow was true and "only the names have been changed to protect the innocent"?

24. Name the screwball wife on CBS's *My Favorite Husband.*

25. What weekly radio series of the early 1950s featured the four lead performers from television's most popular situation comedy, *I Love Lucy*?

26. Who played the part of marshal Matt Dillon on *Gunsmoke*?

27. Whom did Arthur Godfrey fire on the air on October 19, 1953, ostensibly because of his "lack of humility"?

28. Who was host of *The Breakfast Club*?

29. Name Howard Cosell's longest-running ABC radio series.

30. Who played the title role in every episode of the twenty-seven-year network run of *Ma Perkins*?

31. Who were the "battling Bickersons"?

32. What satiric duo created such characters as Wally Ballou, Mary McGoon, and Augustus Winesap?

33. Who were the three men responsible for Britain's *Goon Show* in the 1950s, creating such characters as Minnie Bannister, Eccles, Major Bloodnok, and Neddie Seagoon?

34. When the Beatles landed in New York City in 1964, what local disc jockey spent so much time with them that he was soon known as the "fifth Beatle"?

35. Who was host to a weekly syndicated countdown of the forty biggest hit records in the United States, beginning in 1970, and what was the program called?

36. What 1971 theatrical film starred Clint Eastwood as a late-night disc jockey stalked by a homicidal listener?

37. What syndicated comedy series of the early 1970s included a number of performers who would later turn up in the cast of NBC-TV's *Saturday Night Live*?

38. Who was the original host of *CBS Radio Mystery Theater*?

39. In the opening episode of *The Hitch-Hiker's Guide to the Galaxy,* what happened to the earth?

40. Was there really a WKRP in Cincinnati?

ANSWERS

1. The Mercury Theater's presentation of *"The War of the Worlds"* by *H. G. Wells* on CBS. *What made the drama so convincing was the use of authentic-sounding news bulletins rather than narration and music to carry the first act. People who tuned in after the opening credits came straight into reports of an invasion along the East Coast, blackouts, martial law, and New York City in flames. Though there was a formal break at the end of Act One, a clear identification of the story as a dramatic presentation, and straight voice-over narration in Act Two, people had already panicked. The tense war situation building up in Europe no doubt contributed to listeners' willingness to believe there had been an invasion. (Afterward, some people acknowledged that they thought the Germans, not the Martians, were invading.) Fortunately nobody died in what turned out to be a very effective pre-Halloween scare. In his on-air wrap-up that night, narrator Orson Welles described the episode as "The Mercury Theater's own radio version of dressing up in a sheet and jumping out of a bush and saying boo."*

2. *The ability to "cloud men's minds" through hypnosis, an art he mastered in the Orient. As a result, the Shadow was unseen by those he spoke to, manifesting himself as just a disembodied voice. This was, of course, a perfect radio setup because that was exactly how he came over to listeners at home.*

3. Amos and Andy.

4. *Fireside chats. Roosevelt set them up as a means of speaking to the home audience about his New Deal programs. Beyond that, the broadcasts also served as a reassurance to many listeners, bringing the president of the United States into their homes as a warm, concerned "family" figure.*

5. *The pile of junk precariously balanced inside came crashing*

down on him in a loud clatter, ending with the sound of a tiny bell.
This became a standard routine for the show and produced audience laughter just in anticipation of McGee's actually opening the
door. Sometimes, though, nothing would fall out—but even this was
funny as an unexpected reversal.

6. *In Allen's Alley. Fred Allen's visits to this fictitious street were
among the most popular features on his program.*

7. The Lone Ranger. *The program began in 1933 on Detroit's
WXYZ, a former CBS affiliate that had gone independent under new
management. Within a year, Chicago's WGN and New York's WOR
joined in carrying the new western adventure, and soon the Mutual
radio network was rolling.*

8. *Jack Armstrong, a teen adventurer whose antics actually carried him all around the world, far from Hudson High. The series ran
from 1933 to 1950, with Jim Ameche playing Jack till 1938 and
Charles Flynn carrying the role from 1939 to the end.*

9. *Ovaltine. The Ovaltine shake-up mug was touted as the perfect
way to mix the company's chocolate flavoring with milk. The shaker
served as a mug when the cap was removed. The decoders were far
more fun, especially those offered on the* Captain Midnight *shows,
because they inevitably included a special message for secret
squadron members only.*

10. *Lucky Strike cigarettes. During the early 1940s, another of the
sponsor's routines became almost as familiar as the auctioneer's
chant, namely the slogan "Lucky Strike green has gone to war."
(Green never came back, by the way, and thereafter Lucky Strikes
came in only their red and white package.)*

11. *"Call for Philip Morris!" The line was an inspired plug for Philip
Morris cigarettes. Beginning in 1933, Johnny Roventini repeated it
throughout the broadcast day on various shows sponsored by the
cigarette company, turning the cry into one of the most distinctive
tag lines on the air. In addition, his face popped up in magazine ads
and on billboard signs across the country.*

12. *Frank Sinatra, who performed as part of the Hoboken Four.*

13. *"Thanks for the Memory." Hope traded lines in the song with
co-star Shirley Ross.*

14. The Cinnamon Bear. *The twenty-six-episode fantasy was first presented in 1937 and quickly became a holiday tradition. The series was named after Patty O'Cinnamon, the children's stuffed bear, who came to life and took them to Maybeland in search of the missing Silver Star.*

15. *Arthur Godfrey. Among his shows were* Arthur Godfrey Time *on weekday mornings,* Arthur Godfrey's Talent Scouts *in prime time, and* Arthur Godfrey's Digest *on weekends. When television came along, he simply added video broadcasts to his busy schedule.*

16. *Gertrude Berg, who played Molly Goldberg.*

17. Candid Microphone. *The program had a brief run as a radio series, but scored far better in the 1950s and 1960s on television as* Candid Camera.

18. Blondie. *The program opening followed "Don't touch that dial" with the piercing program identification: "Bl-o-o-o-n-d-i-e-e-e!"*

19. Meet the Press.

20. *The audience shouted his first name—"Groucho!"—welcoming Groucho Marx to another episode of* You Bet Your Life.

21. *"Would you like to be queen for a day?" The audience responded with an enthusiastic "Yes!"*

22. *Connie Brooks on* Our Miss Brooks. *Eve Arden played the high school English teacher as a strong, independent, and intelligent character.*

23. Dragnet. *The program was done in cooperation with the Los Angeles Police Department, drawing on its case files for story hooks.*

24. *Liz Cooper, played by Lucille Ball. The* I Love Lucy *television series came right after this radio program, which ran on CBS from 1948 to 1951, and there were strong elements of Liz Cooper in the character of Lucy Ricardo.*

25. I Love Lucy. *Following the program's tremendous success on television, CBS instituted a radio version with Lucille Ball, Desi Arnaz, William Frawley, and Vivian Vance continuing as the Ricardos and the Mertzes (Lucy and Ricky and Fred and Ethel).*

26. *William Conrad. Though his voice was perfect for the part, when the time came to cast the television version, CBS chose a more traditional western-style performer, James Arness. Nonetheless, Conrad set the style for the role.*

27. *Julius La Rosa. The young singer had apparently broken an unwritten rule that applied to the program's "family" of regulars by arranging his own business deals—hiring an agent and signing an independent recording contract. After performing on Godfrey's morning program that day, La Rosa was left with the warm (but definite) exit line from Arthur Godfrey: "Thanks ever so much, Julie. That was Julie's swan song with us; he goes now out on his own, as his own star."*

28. *Don McNeill.*

29. Speaking of Sports. *Cosell began anchoring the series on June 9, 1956, when it aired as a group of ten five-minute sports roundups slotted only on weekends. By the early 1980s the series consisted of two five-minute commentaries that aired twice a day on weekdays.*

30. *Virginia Payne. She was fifty when the series ended in 1960.*

31. *Don Ameche as John Bickerson and Frances Langford as Blanche Bickerson were husband-and-wife sparring partners caught in a never-ending series of arguments. Their exchanges appeared as part of a number of programs, including their own, from the mid-1940s to the early 1950s.*

32. *Bob Elliott and Ray Goulding, better known as Bob and Ray.*

33. *Spike Milligan, Peter Sellers, and Harry Secombe. The series was originally produced in the 1950s for the BBC and ever since has been rerun in Britain and in syndication in the United States, usually on public radio stations.*

34. *Murray the K of station WINS.*

35. *Casey Kasem, host of* American Top 40. *Kasem was a disc jockey and occasional character actor who started the syndicated show in 1970 as the perfect package for his storehouse of pop history, which he used to provide background on the latest top forty hits. Beginning in 1980 he syndicated a video version as well,* America's Top 10.

36. Play Misty for Me. *"Misty" was the song the would-be killer always phoned in as a request on the late night shift.*

37. The National Lampoon Radio Hour. *Creative personnel on this series turned up both on camera and behind the scenes in NBC's popular* Saturday Night Live. *They included John Belushi, Chevy Chase, Bill Murray, Brian Doyle-Murray, Michael O'Donoghue, Gilda Radner, and producer Bob Tischler.*

38. *E. G. Marshall. This first important radio drama series in more than a decade began as a seven-night-a-week program on January 6, 1974. After six years, the show cut back to a Monday-through-Friday schedule and soon thereafter Tammy Grimes replaced Marshall as host. The series ended on December 31, 1982.*

39. *The earth was totally demolished by an alien wrecking fleet to make room for a new hyperspace bypass. The hero of the series, Arthur Dent (played by Simon Jones), was rescued from the destruction at the last moment when one of his friends confessed that he was an alien and, more important, that he knew how they could both escape. They hitched a ride on one of the spaceships in the demolition fleet. Their subsequent adventures together first played on Britain's BBC in 1978 and on National Public Radio in the United States in 1981.*

40. *No. However, there was a WKRC in Cincinnati. Once the* WKRP *television series caught on, a radio station in Dallas, Georgia, received permission from the FCC to change its call letters to WKRP in September 1979.*

THE PIONEER AGE
Station Call Letters
Radio Firsts
Pioneer Review

Station Call Letters

For each of the following stations, state what the call letters originally stood for:

1. WGBS in New York.
2. WGN in Chicago.
3. WLS in Chicago.
4. WABC in New York.
5. WCNN in Atlanta.

ANSWERS

1. *WGBS stood for Gimbel Brothers' Store, a large department store in New York City.*

2. *WGN stood for World's Greatest Newspaper and was run by the Chicago Tribune's company.*

3. *WLS stood for World's Largest Store and was run by Sears Roebuck, a Chicago-based department store that distributed its shop-at-home catalogs throughout the country—thus the claim "the world's largest store."*

4. *WABC stood for the Atlantic Broadcasting Company, a corporation formed in 1926 to take over WAHG in New York from Alfred H. Grebe. CBS later bought WABC from Atlantic Broadcasting and changed the call letters to WCBS. In 1953, the American Broadcasting Company (formerly the Blue network) reactivated the WABC call letters as the new identification for its New York station, WJZ.*

5. *WCNN stood for Cable News Network. In 1982, when WRNG in Atlanta began carrying a radio version of Ted Turner's all-news service for cable television, it adopted the CNN call letters.*

Radio Firsts

1. Where did the first ad for a radio set appear?

2. What was the first championship boxing match broadcast on radio?

3. Who won the first major league baseball game broadcast on radio?

4. When was the first World Series contest broadcast over radio?

5. What was the first presidential election in which returns were broadcast on radio?

6. Who was the first American president to speak over radio?

7. What were the first operas broadcast by radio from the Metropolitan Opera House in New York?

8. What was the first "network" of radio stations?

9. What was the first national political convention carried on radio?

10. What was the first regularly sponsored network series?

ANSWERS

1. *In Scientific American's January 13, 1906, issue. The sets were offered by New York radio pioneer Hugo Gernsbeck.*

2. *The July 2, 1921, match in Jersey City between Jack Dempsey and George Carpentier. O. J. Smith described the action over RCA's first radio station, WJY in Hoboken. Dempsey KO'd Carpentier in the fourth round.*

3. *The Pittsburgh Pirates. They defeated the Philadelphia Phillies 8 to 5 on August 5, 1921, in a game carried over KDKA in Pittsburgh.*

4. *On October 5, 1921, studio announcer Thomas H. Cowan read reports relayed to him from a Newark Sun reporter attending the series opener between the New York Yankees and the New York Giants at the Polo Grounds in New York. Cowan's descriptions were transmitted by WJZ, Westinghouse's four-day-old station in Newark, New Jersey. The following year, Graham McNamee did the first World Series radio broadcast directly from the ball park, covering the October 7 opener between the same two teams at the same stadium.*

5. *The Woodrow Wilson–Charles Evans Hughes election of November 7, 1916. Lee DeForest, who had set up America's first regular broadcast operation in February 1907, broadcast returns on election night from his "studio" in the New York American Hotel in the Bronx. He incorrectly reported that Republican Hughes had defeated President Wilson.*

6. *Woodrow Wilson. His speech upon returning from Europe was broadcast by a U.S. Navy–operated station on July 4, 1919. President Warren Harding was the first chief executive to broadcast over a privately owned station, speaking at the dedication of the Francis*

Scott Key memorial at Fort McHenry in Baltimore on June 14, 1922. Baltimore station WEAR (later WFBR) carried it.

7. Pagliacci *and* Cavalleria Rusticana. *They were sung by Enrico Caruso on January 13, 1910, and broadcast by Lee DeForest from his vanguard radio station set up in the Parker Building in New York City.*

8. *An ad hoc hookup between Westinghouse's Newark, New Jersey, station, WJZ, and General Electric's Schenectady, New York, station, WGY, on October 7, 1922, for the broadcast of that day's opening game in the World Series. In the months thereafter, there were other occasional hookups between stations, but the first regular system of station connection began on July 1, 1923, when WMAF in South Dartmouth, Massachusetts, began regularly broadcasting programs fed out via cable from AT&T's New York station, WEAF. In little more than a year, approximately twenty-five other stations joined this unofficial AT&T network. However, the first formal network was NBC, the National Broadcasting Company, which was set up by RCA to take over AT&T's radio operations on November 15, 1926. Over this setup, NBC's first programming was carried by twenty-five stations in twenty-one cities, as far west as Kansas City.*

9. *The Republican convention that opened on June 10, 1924, in Cleveland. Graham McNamee anchored the coverage over fifteen stations on AT&T's ad hoc network, which stretched from Boston to Kansas City. At the convention, President Calvin Coolidge was nominated for another term.*

10. The Eveready Hour. *The program premiered on December 4, 1923, on AT&T's WEAF as the first important variety series in radio history. On February 12, 1924, Eveready began sponsoring the show on two other stations, which carried the program via cable.*

Pioneer Review

1. What colors were associated with NBC's radio networks from the 1920s to the 1940s?

2. For more than two years prior to *Amos and Andy,* that show's creators played another ethnic pair. Name the previous show, which ran locally on Chicago's WGN.

3. Who was host to network radio's first major variety hour, beginning October 24, 1929, on NBC?

4. Who played the title role in Texaco's 1932 *Fire Chief* comedy show?

5. Name the two major radio ratings services of the 1930s and 1940s.

6. Name the oldest continuously operating radio station in the United States.

7. Beginning August 28, 1922, WEAF in New York presented the first regularly sponsored programming on radio. What are the current call letters of that pioneer station?

8. What was the first FM station?

9. What was CBS's original New York City affiliate when it began broadcasting in 1927?

10. One of NBC's pioneer programs aimed at young listeners was *Coast to Coast on a Bus,* which ran on Sunday mornings beginning in the late 1920s. Who was the host?

11. What was the original name of the *Grand Ole Opry*?

12. Who was responsible for the first popular disc jockey show on a major radio station?

13. What was the first major network series to originate from Los Angeles?

14. What radio adventure series was based on the exploits of a real cowboy who had been a silent film star in the 1920s?

15. Which major university had its own network program for nearly fifty years?

ANSWERS

1. *Red, blue, and orange. Soon after NBC began programming in November 1926, it set up two separate services, the Red network and the Blue network, which broadcast different programs to different stations. According to one NBC legend, the names came from the colors of the pins stuck into a map of the United States that network executives used to plan the national hookups. Another story has it that the telephone company used the red and blue color codes back in the 1920s to distinguish the wiring connections for the two network services. In any case, the red and blue designations took hold almost immediately, so it was only natural to use another color (orange) to designate NBC's stations on the West Coast, which were connected to each other but not yet hooked into the rest of the network. During the 1930s the separate orange identification became unnecessary, as the entire country was wired. The Blue network became ABC in the mid-1940s making the separate Red designation unnecessary as well.*

2. Sam and Henry. *Freeman Gosden and Charles Correll did that program from 1926 to 1928 before moving on to Chicago's WMAQ with* Amos and Andy. WGN, *meanwhile, continued the popular* Sam and Henry *show without them.*

3. *Rudy Vallee, a popular young crooner of the 1920s. His pioneer* Fleischmann Hour *gave listeners a taste of big-time vaudeville entertainment and quickly became one of radio's first major hits.*

4. *Ed Wynn. He even appeared in a fire chief's costume while doing the show, though that was not necessary for a radio performance. Nonetheless, Wynn had strong vaudeville roots, and the costume no doubt helped him feel more comfortable before the radio mike.*

5. *The Crossleys and the Hoopers. The Crossley ratings service* began in 1930, soon after the start of network radio, but was soon overshadowed in the mid-1930s by the Hooper organization. The Hooper service began its operations in 1935 and was bought out by the Nielsen company fifteen years later, in 1950.

6. *KCBS in San Francisco.* In the spring of 1909, Dr. Charles Herrold of the San Jose College of Engineering began a weekly half-hour series of broadcasts to twenty friends he had given crystal receiving sets. In 1912, under the call letters SJN, the broadcasts went on a daily schedule. In 1920, the station adopted a religious format and soon thereafter took the new call letters KQW. In 1925 the station became a commercial radio service and, in 1949, changed its call letters to KCBS.

7. *WNBC.* On July 25, 1922, the American Telephone and Telegraph Company set up its New York station as WBAY. That became WEAF on August 16, 1922, and soon began to present commercial broadcasts. It was sold to RCA on November 15, 1926, when it became the flagship station of the new NBC network. On November 1, 1946, WEAF changed its call letters to WNBC. On October 18, 1954, WNBC became WRCA, but then changed back to WNBC on May 23, 1960.

8. *WGTR.* Actually, the first public demonstration of FM radio took place at a meeting of the Institute of Radio Engineers in November 1935 over W2AG in Yonkers, New York. It was conducted by inventor E. H. Armstrong. However, the first FM station licensed by the FCC was W1XOJ in Paxton, Massachusetts, which began construction in August 1937 and went on the air in May 1939 as W43B. It later changed its call letters to WGTR. Meanwhile, Armstrong's FM station, W2XMN in Alpine, New Jersey, also went on the air in 1939. The first commercial FM station was WSM-FM in Nashville, which began operations in 1941.

9. *WOR.* The station was one of the eighteen original CBS affiliates that aired the network's premiere programming on September 18, 1927. CBS, however, soon decided to set up its own flagship station for the vital New York City market. On January 8, 1929, CBS bought WABC from the Atlantic Broadcasting Company, and WABC began sharing CBS shows with WOR until WOR's affiliate contract with CBS expired on September 2, 1929. WABC changed its call letters to WCBS on November 1, 1946.

10. *Milton Cross. Each week he welcomed a talented crew of young performers who sang and acted in skits while aboard the White Rabbit transportation line. The series ran for fifteen years.*

11. The WSM Barn Dance. *The program premiered on WSM in Nashville on November 28, 1925. By early 1926 the show's host, George D. Hay, had begun calling it the* Grand Ole Opry, *and the name stuck.*

12. *Martin Block on WNEW in New York. In February 1935, during lulls in the extensive radio coverage of the trial of Bruno Richard Hauptmann for the kidnap death of the son of Charles Lindbergh, Block presented a show he called* Make Believe Ballroom. *During that program he played records of band music in sets similar to those a live band might play. Before then, virtually all music on the radio was live, either from studios or from dance halls. Block's program was so popular that it remained on after the Hauptmann trial ended.*

13. Forty-Five Minutes in Hollywood. *The series, which began in February 1934 on CBS, dramatized upcoming feature films.*

14. Tom Mix. *Following his film career, the real-life Tom Mix lent his name to the radio series, which began in 1933, but he never appeared on it. After a few seasons, the program put aside recreating Mix's personal adventures and developed his fictional persona to a much greater degree. He became the hero of what was touted as "radio's biggest western detective program," presenting contemporary western adventures. During World War II Mix was a full-time fighter for the Allies on the home front.*

15. *Northwestern University in Evanston, Illinois.* Northwestern Reviewing Stand, *a weekly interview and discussion program, began as a local Chicago program in October 1933, was picked up by the Mutual network in 1935, and continued into the 1980s.*

THEME SONGS

Theme Songs

Name the performer or character associated with each of the following theme songs:

1. The *William Tell* Overture.
2. "Flight of the Bumble Bee."
3. "Back in the Saddle Again."
4. "Happy Trails."
5. "Love Nest."
6. "Love in Bloom."
7. "My Time Is Your Time."
8. "Polly Wolly Doodle."
9. "Red River Valley."
10. "When the Blue of the Night Meets the Gold of the Day."
11. "Moonlight Serenade."
12. "Rhapsody in Blue."
13. "Inka Dinka Doo."

ANSWERS

1. *The Lone Ranger.*
2. *The Green Hornet.*
3. *Gene Autry.*
4. *Roy Rogers.*
5. *George Burns and Gracie Allen.*
6. *Jack Benny.*
7. *Rudy Vallee.*
8. *Just Plain Bill.*
9. *Our Gal Sunday.*
10. *Bing Crosby.*
11. *Glenn Miller and his orchestra.*
12. *Paul Whiteman and his orchestra.*
13. *Jimmy Durante.*

THE GOLDEN AGE
Comedy and Variety
Variety and Music
Police and Private Eyes
Adventure Heroes
Mystery, Suspense, and Drama
Soap Operas
Games and Quizzes
Golden Review

Comedy and Variety

1. Milton Berle starred in two radio series, *Kiss and Make Up* and *At Home with the Berles,* just before he went over to television in 1948, where he became the first video superstar. What was the chief difference between Berle on radio and Berle on TV?

2. On *Amos and Andy,* who played Amos, Andy, and the Kingfish?

3. Who played the impish seven-year-old girl known as Baby Snooks?

4. Prior to receiving their own program, Ozzie and Harriet Nelson worked for three years as musical and comedy backup for what comedy-variety star?

5. Unlike most of the key performers in *The Adventures of Ozzie and Harriet,* Tommy Bernard and Henry Blair stayed with their roles for less than half the program's ten-year radio run. Why?

6. What roles did Don Wilson, Dennis Day, and Phil Harris play on *The Jack Benny Program*?

7. What did Jack Benny's violin teacher, the Maxwell roadster, and the train station announcer have in common?

8. According to program legend, whom did Jack Benny meet at the May Company Department Store's hosiery counter in Los Angeles?

[31]

9. Who was judge for the 1945 "I Can't Stand Jack Benny Because—" contest?

10. The series *A Day in the Life of Dennis Day* focused on a character named Dennis Day, a soda jerk who felt that he could sing as well as the Dennis Day who appeared on Jack Benny's show. Who played the title character on this *Dennis Day* series?

11. Who staged a comic campaign for president of the United States in 1940, running as a candidate on the Surprise party ticket?

12. Who spoke the malapropisms on *The Easy Aces*?

13. Clancy the cop, Eddie the waiter, and Archie the barkeep were all familiar characters on what 1940s comedy show?

14. Did Duffy ever show up at *Duffy's Tavern*?

15. Who was the pompous next-door neighbor who constantly locked horns with Fibber McGee in the early 1940s?

16. Until the fall of 1947 what was the most incongruous aspect of the character of Beulah, a big, warm-hearted black maid?

17. *The Great Gildersleeve* and *Beulah* were spin-offs from what other series?

18. Who were the satiric "gloom chasers" of the 1930s, a duo specializing in radio parody and wordplay?

19. Name the popular American humorist featured on *The Gulf Show* from its premiere in 1933 until his death in 1935.

20. What sit-com couple of the 1930s lived in the small town of Crooper, Illinois, with their young son Rush, Uncle Fletcher, and such colorful friends and neighbors as Chuck and Dottie Brainfeeble, Smelly Clark, and Rishigan Fishigan from Sishigan, Michigan?

21. Who were the co-owners and operators of the Jot 'Em Down Store in Pine Ridge, Arkansas?

22. Who played old Ben Willet, owner of a general store in a tiny West Coast town, on the 1940s series *Point Sublime*?

23. Who was the nervous door-to-door salesman (created in the late 1920s by Al Pearce) who was afraid to talk to people?

24. What 1930s comedy-variety star had as one of his catch phrases, "Vas you dere, Sharlie?"?

25. What did the Mad Russian say in greeting people on *The Eddie Cantor Show*?

26. Name one of Bob Hope's wildest sidemen, a character who had a booming voice, a large dark mustache, and the nickname "Professor."

27. What 1940s sit-com featured the adventures of a pigtailed hillbilly girl living in the big city?

28. Who played the part of Pedro, the silly Mexican handyman on *The Judy Canova Show*?

29. Harry Einstein, one of the regulars on *The Eddie Cantor Show*, was best known for his humorous characterization of a Greek immigrant. What was he called?

30. The Aldrich family was first introduced to radio audiences during 1938 in a series of skits on what popular variety series?

31. What teenage comedy featured the antics of Judy Foster and her boyfriend Oogie Pringle?

32. What teenage comedy featured the antics of Corliss Archer and her boyfriend Dexter Franklin?

33. What 1940s sit-com featured Ann Sothern in the part of an outspoken Brooklyn beauty?

34. What comedy series featured the adventures of an Italian immigrant living in Chicago, with J. Carroll Naish in the title role, Alan Reed as a father desperate to marry off his fat daughter, and Hans Conried as a crusty German immigrant attending night school?

35. On *The Life of Riley,* what job did Riley's friend Digby "Digger" O'Dell have?

36. What late 1940s sit-com featured the level-headed Jane Stacy narrating the adventures of her logically illogical friend and roommate?

37. Who played the role of Irma Peterson in *My Friend Irma* for seven years on radio, three years on television, and in a pair of theatrical films?

38. In September 1950 there was an important cast change in *The Great Gildersleeve.* What happened?

39. Name the early 1950s comedy featuring Spring Byington as Lily Ruskin, a widow living with her daughter and son-in-law.

40. On *Our Miss Brooks,* who played the blustery principal of Madison High School?

ANSWERS

1. *Berle was a flop on radio. He had built his reputation chiefly from nightclub routines that showcased his strong visual humor, which radio could not convey. Thus, he was an ideal choice as host of one of NBC's first television variety shows,* Texaco Star Theater, *even though he had been only an average radio personality. Both* Kiss and Make Up *(in 1946) and* At Home with the Berles *(in 1947) reflected these limitations for radio. The first was a quiz show modeled after* You Bet Your Life, *and the second was a simple domestic sit-com with Berle as the father and Arnold Stang as his son.*

2. *The creators of the series, Freeman Gosden and Charles Correll. Correll played Andy Brown while Gosden took the roles of Amos Jones and George "Kingfish" Stevens.*

3. *Fanny Brice. She created the character in the early 1920s, but did not really use it until the following decade. Then Baby Snooks served as the basis for a whole new career for Brice, who turned the character into a successful radio favorite from the mid-1930s into the 1950s.*

4. *Red Skelton. Harriet Hilliard was the vocalist with Ozzie Nelson's band, which supplied the music for* The Red Skelton Show, *along with some light husband-and-wife transitional banter. Harriet also stepped into various skits in such roles as mother to Skelton's "mean widdle kid" character and Daisy June, Clem Kadiddlehopper's girl friend.*

5. *They were no longer needed in the roles of Dave and Rick Nelson. When Ozzie and Harriet's program first began in 1944, the couple's real-life children were only eight (Dave) and four (Rick), so Tommy Bernard and Henry Blair came in to play the parts. Four years later, the Nelsons decided to allow Dave and Rick to join the show playing themselves. They took over the roles beginning in early 1949, replacing Bernard and Blair.*

6. *Themselves. Because* The Jack Benny Program *included action "behind the scenes" in preparation for each week's show, this was a perfectly natural move. Thus, some characters such as program announcer Don Wilson, singer Dennis Day, and bandleader Phil Harris simply played character exaggerations of themselves, not even changing their names.*

7. *The voice of Mel Blanc. On* The Jack Benny Program, *the versatile Blanc handled not only character roles such as Professor La Blanc (Benny's violin teacher) and the brassy train announcer, but also special sound effects such as the sputtering old Maxwell automobile.*

8. *His future wife, Sadie Marks, later appearing on the air in the role of Mary Livingstone, Jack's girl friend. Their meeting at the May Company took place in real life in 1926 and became one of the running gags on* The Jack Benny Program. *They were married in 1927.*

9. *Fred Allen (of course), with whom Benny carried on an on-air "feud" for years.*

10. *The real Dennis Day, of course. The program ran for five seasons, from 1946 to 1951. Day continued to appear on Jack Benny's program as well, playing that "other" Dennis Day.*

11. *Gracie Allen. As part of her campaign, Gracie wrote an article for* Liberty *magazine explaining why a woman should be president. She and George Burns even went so far as to schedule a mock party convention in Omaha, Nebraska, on May 15–18, 1940.*

12. *Jane Ace. She and her husband Goodman Ace worked the simple format of a conversation around a card table into a comedy success that lasted more than a decade. Jane's comical confusion of words and phrases (such as "Time wounds all heels") were particularly sharp and effective in this context.*

13. *Duffy's Tavern. Clancy was the neighborhood cop on the beat, Eddie was a waiter at the tavern-restaurant, and Archie was its manager. Other regulars included Miss Duffy, the owner's daughter, Clifton Finnegan, the quintessential dumb lug, and his brother Wilfred.*

14. *Duffy never turned up at his own tavern, though he often telephoned his head barkeep, Archie. This resulted in the running gag in which Archie answered the telephone saying, "Hello, Duffy's Tavern, where the elite meet to eat. Archie the manager speaking. Duffy ain't here—oh, hello, Duffy."*

15. *Throckmorton P. Gildersleeve, played by Harold Peary.*

16. *The character was played by a white man. Marlin Hurt created Beulah in the early 1940s and did the booming falsetto voice himself until his death in 1946. Another white man, Bob Corley, briefly succeeded him in 1947 before Hattie McDaniel, a popular black film performer, took over the role.*

17. Fibber McGee and Molly. The Great Gildersleeve *series began in the fall of 1941, and* Beulah *started in July 1945. Actually, Marlin Hurt had played Beulah on other shows prior to joining* Fibber McGee and Molly, *but the tremendous boost provided by that program resulted in the spin-off series. Throckmorton P. Gildersleeve, however, was expressly created as a foil to Fibber McGee and had become quite popular when he began his own series.*

18. *Frederick Chase Taylor and Budd Hulick, better known as Stoopnagle and Budd. Their first network program was* The Gloom Chasers *beginning in 1931, and they subsequently appeared as a team on a number of other shows throughout the decade, including Fred Allen's* Town Hall Tonight. *They split up in 1938.*

19. *Will Rogers. He died in a plane crash on August 15, 1935.*

20. *Vic and Sade. During the 1930s, the only three characters who actually appeared on mike were Vic, Sade, and Rush. In the 1940s, though, the show opened up a bit with the addition of other voices, most notably that of Clarence Hartzell as Uncle Fletcher.*

21. *Lum Edwards and Abner Peabody, played by Chester Lauck and Norris Goff. The two performers created the setting for* Lum and Abner *as the perfect spot for their hillbilly characters to gather and play checkers, exchange stories, and become involved in various money-making schemes.*

22. *Cliff Arquette. There were fewer than a thousand people in the town and, naturally, Ben Willet's store was the gathering spot for gossip and conversation.*

23. *Elmer Blurt. On* Al Pearce and His Gang *in the 1930s and 1940s, the character would knock on the door and mumble, "Nobody home, I hope, I hope, I hope."*

24. *Jack Pearl in his popular Baron von Munchausen character. He would use the line whenever questioned about a particularly tall tale describing his "heroic" exploits.*

25. *"How dooo you dooo?" That popular character was created and played by one of the program's regulars, Bert Gordon.*

26. *Jerry Colonna.*

27. The Judy Canova Show.

28. *Mel Blanc. As Pedro he would interrupt other cast members with the catch phrase, "Pardon me for talkin' en your face!"*

29. *Nick Parkyakarkas. In the mid-1940s the character was featured in his own show,* Meet Me at Parky's, *a sit-com set at his Greek restaurant.*

30. *Rudy Vallee's variety program. In the summer of 1939,* The Aldrich Family *premiered as a separate show.*

31. A Date with Judy. *The series began in 1942 as a summer replacement for Bob Hope and ended its run in 1950. Richard Crenna served a stint as boyfriend Oogie.*

32. Meet Corliss Archer. *The series began in 1943 and ended its radio run in 1955. The show was based on F. Hugh Herbert's play* Kiss and Tell *and also ran as an early 1950s television series.*

33. *Maisie. The program, based on a series of theatrical films from MGM, played on radio from 1945 to 1949, beginning on CBS and ending in syndication. Ann Sothern stayed in the leading role of Maisie Revere throughout the run, though there were some format variations along the way. Initially, Maisie was a worldly-wise traveler, whereas in the syndicated version she spent her time Stateside.*

34. Life with Luigi. *J. Carroll Naish played Luigi Basko, an Italian immigrant; Alan Reed was Pasquale, a restaurant owner who had been Luigi's sponsor to America, in the hope that marriage between his daughter Rosa and Luigi would take place; and Hans Conried* was Schultz, a fellow student at the night school Luigi attended in the hope of becoming an American citizen. Every week, Luigi would describe his latest escapades in a letter to his "Mama Mia" back home in Italy. The show began in 1948 and ran until 1953.

35. *He was an undertaker. This led to the inevitable run of burial jokes, such as O'Dell's exit line, "I'd better be shoveling off."*

36. My Friend Irma, *which played on CBS from 1947 to 1954.*

37. *Marie Wilson. She played Irma Peterson as a sexy, attractive woman who existed on another plane of reality. Operating in much the same manner as Gracie Allen, Irma brought her own unique interpretations to otherwise harmless everyday words and actions.*

38. *There was a new performer in the leading role of Throckmorton P. Gildersleeve. Harold Peary, who had created the character on the* Fibber McGee and Molly Show *more than a decade before, decided to leave the series to start a new show. Surprisingly, Peary's successor, Willard Waterman, was so effective a replacement that he not only finished out the radio run of the series, but also assumed the role for a 1955 syndicated TV version.*

39. December Bride. *A television version of the series began in 1954 with Spring Byington continuing the role of Lily.*

40. *Gale Gordon as Osgood Conklin.*

Variety and Music

1. Name the two big hit Saturday night country music shows of the 1930s and 1940s, one based in Chicago, the other in Nashville.

2. Who was the easygoing host of *The Kraft Music Hall* during its heyday from 1935 to 1946?

3. What variety show host gave Edgar Bergen and Charlie McCarthy their big break, turning them into an "overnight" success on December 17, 1936?

4. What seemed so amazing about the success of Edgar Bergen as a radio performer?

5. Name two other wooden dummies that Edgar Bergen used on his show. One was the program's slow-talking, dumb sidekick; the other was a "man-hungry old maid."

6. In 1942 and 1943, Shirley Dinsdale and Paul Winchell followed the radio trail blazed by Edgar Bergen and Charlie McCarthy. Who were the wooden companions to these two radio newcomers?

7. In early 1943, vaudeville veteran Jimmy Durante began his successful radio career when he teamed up with what young comic?

8. What CBS variety program replaced the *American School of the Air* as an unsponsored summer filler in 1945 and ended up staying on the air for twenty-seven years?

9. Who were the Happiness Boys, and how did they get their nickname?

10. Novelty performer Merwyn Bogue was better known to 1930s fans of Kay Kyser by his stage name. What was it?

11. What bandleader led his satirical City Slickers through parodies of operas and modern musicals and even created a 1942 novelty hit called "Der Fuehrer's Face"?

12. The host of the 1944 CBS variety series *Let Yourself Go* was touted in the opening as "the fella who let himself go and became Ziegfeld's biggest folly." Name him.

13. The 1935 *Shell Chateau* series on NBC was built around what veteran down-on-one-knee vaudeville singer and comic?

14. Shortly after Bing Crosby began on CBS in 1931, NBC countered with its own new crooner. Who was he?

15. Who was the featured singer on *The Camel Quarter Hour* and *The Coke Club*?

16. What musical show took listeners on a weekly whirlwind "tour" of New York's leading nightclubs to hear the top tunes of the week?

17. What popular female vocalist received a big boost in the early 1940s as a regular on *The Chamber Music Society of Lower Basin Street*?

18. What was unusual about the twenty-two-piece orchestra used on the mid-1930s' *Hour of Charm*?

19. Who led one of the largest orchestra and chorus combinations on radio, beginning in 1932 with a fifty-five-member assembly?

20. In December 1937, NBC presented the first radio concert by the newly formed NBC Symphony Orchestra. Who was the conductor?

21. Name the NBC announcer who served as the Voice of the Met, providing background commentary on and introductions to the radio broadcasts of New York's Metropolitan Opera from the 1930s until his death in 1975.

22. What radio veteran served as maestro of the *Bell Telephone Hour* from its premiere in 1940, conducted the orchestra, and even composed the program's theme?

23. What popular singer jumped to CBS's *Palmolive Beauty Box Theater* in 1937 after seven years as the big draw on NBC's *Cities Service Concerts*?

24. Who were the hosts of the 1940s musical *Eight-to-the-Bar Ranch* series?

25. What was Kate Smith's theme song, and what was the opening line of her 1930s programs?

26. Name the patriotic song introduced by Kate Smith on Armistice Day, 1938.

27. How did the weekly *Your Hit Parade* determine its ranking of the most popular songs in the nation?

28. On the February 10, 1942, episode of Glenn Miller's radio program, RCA Victor presented the popular bandleader with the entertainment industry's first solid gold record. What recording earned Miller that honor?

ANSWERS

1. The National Barn Dance *and* The Grand Ole Opry. *Both were done live at auditoriums in their respective cities (Chicago and Nashville), with the music continuing long after the radio broadcast had ended.* The National Barn Dance *ran from 1924 to the early 1950s, while* The Grand Ole Opry *kept right on going from 1925 into the 1980s.*

2. *Bing Crosby.*

3. *Rudy Vallee, who made a point of trying to uncover new talent. He had Bergen and McCarthy do a guest spot on his variety show and, when that went over well, brought them back many times over the next few months. In the late spring of 1937, Bergen and McCarthy began their own series.*

4. *He was a ventriloquist, a type of performer who would seem to require a visual contact with the audience not possible on radio. Yet Bergen quickly demonstrated that his real skill as a ventriloquist went beyond simple visual tricks; he developed the personalities of his dummies so effectively that they became real-life characters over the air.*

5. *Mortimer Snerd was the dumb sidekick, and Effie Klinker was the man-hungry old maid.*

6. *Shirley Dinsdale had Judy Splinters, and Paul Winchell worked with Jerry Mahoney. Neither could match the radio success of Bergen and McCarthy, though Winchell and Mahoney became quite successful during the next decade as television stars.*

7. *Garry Moore. Though Durante and Moore were more than two decades apart in age, they somehow clicked together as a smooth musical comedy team. Durante even referred to Moore as "Junior." They stayed together four seasons, then pursued successful solo radio careers.*

8. Arthur Godfrey Time. *Godfrey had been a local radio personality in Washington, D.C., since the early 1930s, and had even been the host of a brief network series for Mutual. He built a reputation in New York during the early 1940s through syndication of his morning program. Godfrey was considered a risky investment by advertisers, however, because he poked gentle fun at their overblown commercial copy on the air. As a result, when he began on the CBS network in 1945, he had no sponsors. Nonetheless, he quickly caught on with the national audience, won some commercial support, and kept the morning time period into the fall of 1945 as a result. In the process, the returning American School of the Air had to take its classes to the afternoon.*

9. *Billy Jones and Ernie Hare. They sang and did light comedy on the radio for nearly two decades, receiving their Happiness Boys moniker in the mid-1920s when they hosted a weekly show for Happiness candy. Though subsequent sponsors attempted to attach their names to the act, none of the others stuck. Best Foods dubbed them the Best Foods Boys, Tastyeast Bakers tried the Tasty Breadwinners, and Interwoven Socks called them the Interwoven Pair.*

10. *Ish Kabibble.*

11. *Spike Jones. He and his City Slickers performed primarily as guest artists on radio through the 1940s, though they had their own series, which ran for two seasons on CBS beginning in 1947.*

12. *Milton Berle.*

13. *Al Jolson, best known for his rendition of "Mammy."*

14. *Russ Columbo.*

15. *Morton Downey, who was one of the highest paid singers of the 1930s. The crooning tenor also appeared in numerous special radio broadcasts, including some beamed overseas. This was particularly appropriate for Downey because he had built quite a reputation in the late 1920s and early 1930s performing in Europe.*

16. The Manhattan Merry-Go-Round. *The program ran from the early 1930s to the late 1940s but, of course, never actually went to any of the nightclubs it visited on the air. Like any other musical variety show, it was all done from the studio.*

17. *Dinah Shore.*

18. *All the members were women. Male orchestra leader Phil Spitalny had conducted an extensive cross-country talent search in the early 1930s for the purpose of putting together a top-notch group of female musicians, and, in January 1935, he began his program featuring them.* The Hour of Charm *was a success and played for more than ten years. Eventually he married one of the members of the orchestra.*

19. *Fred Waring. He created a distinctive "glee club" that gave his orchestra a unique sound no one else could offer. It was also one of the most expensive orchestra acts on radio, with well over fifty people on the payroll most of the time. Nonetheless, Waring performed successfully on radio for two decades and made a smooth transition into early television as well.*

20. *Arturo Toscanini. That first broadcast included works by Vivaldi, Mozart, and Brahms and marked the beginning of the conductor's seventeen-year association with NBC—one that carried right on through to television.*

21. *Milton Cross.*

22. *Donald Voorhees.*

23. *Jessica Dragonette. After less than a year, though, she eased out of broadcasting to concentrate on personal appearance concert tours. Thereafter she chiefly made only guest shots on radio.*

24. *The Andrews Sisters (LaVerne, Maxine, and Patti). The program premiered in late 1944.*

25. *"When the Moon Comes over the Mountain," accompanied by the simple greeting, "Hello, everybody, this is Kate Smith."*

26. *"God Bless America" by Irving Berlin. Kate Smith sang it virtually every week on her show throughout World War II.*

27. *Program creator George Hill set up an elaborate system to survey the relative popularity of the latest hits, using a large staff to do the job each week. They checked sales at selected record shops and sheet music stores throughout the country, looked at jukebox play, and asked radio stations and bandleaders what their most requested*

*numbers were. Number one on the first edition of the program
(April 20, 1935): the Rodgers and Hart number, "Soon."*

28. *"Chattanooga Choo Choo," which sold more than 1,200,000
copies. The award was a recording of the song actually pressed on
solid gold.*

Police and Private Eyes

1. From 1939 to 1946, *Sherlock Holmes* had its most successful run as a network radio series. Who played Holmes and
   Dr. Watson in this version?

2. Who played Sergeant Joe Friday of the Los Angeles Police Department?

3. Who was Joe Friday's original partner on *Dragnet*?

4. What detective series stopped the action near the end of
   the story and turned to a panel of "armchair detectives"
   for suggested solutions?

5. Name the 1946 hard-boiled detective series featuring
   Howard Duff in the title role.

6. What detective series used expense account items as
   jumping-off points for scenes in each week's case?

7. Name the stout detective who preferred eating gourmet
   food and raising orchids to crime fighting, yet still managed to solve his share of baffling mysteries and murders.

8. Name the lighthearted husband-and-wife detective team
   (and their pet dog) featured in *The Thin Man* series.

9. Name the Dashiell Hammett detective character created
   especially for radio as a delightful twist on Hammett's own
   Thin Man.

10. Who played sophisticated private detective Richard Dia-
    mond?

11. In the late 1940s, Vincent Price assumed the title role in the international adventures of what "Robin Hood of modern crime"?

12. The popular 1950 film *The Third Man* also had a syndicated radio counterpart at the time. Who carried on the larcenous adventures of Harry Lime in this series?

13. Who were the co-stars of the early 1950s syndicated adventure series, *Bold Venture,* set in Havana, Cuba?

14. In the summer of 1951, Jack Webb starred in a short-run crime series set at a speakeasy during Prohibition. Name the show.

15. Both *Johnny Madero, Pier 23* and *Pat Novak, for Hire* featured tough-talking characters who offered boats for rent on the San Francisco waterfront and inevitably stumbled across murder. Who played the lead in both series?

16. What nineteenth-century pulp detective came to radio in 1943 and was touted in the program opening as "the most famous of all manhunters, the detective whose ability at solving crime is unequalled in the history of detective fiction"?

17. What long-running crime series used as its opening theme a selection from Sergei Prokofiev's *Love for Three Oranges?*

18. Who played the female detective title character in the 1946 *Affairs of Ann Scotland* series?

19. Name the beautiful San Francisco detective who could be reached by dialing YUkon 2-8209.

20. What 1949 crime series followed detective Danny Clover, a New York policeman assigned to cover the Broadway beat?

21. What private detective was billed as "enemy to those who make him an enemy, friend to those who have no friends"?

22. What 1940s crime series featured a criminal who reformed when he lost his memory, became a doctor, and
then (with his memory restored) specialized in trying to
help capture and rehabilitate other criminals?

23. What detective tossed out silver dollars as tips to doormen
and such during his investigations?

24. What was the gimmick used by the detective hero of the
1948–1952 CBS crime series *Mr. Chameleon*?

25. What detective was billed as the "tracer of lost persons"?

26. Gem Blades, sponsor of *The Falcon* detective series during the mid-1940s, included an appropriately ominous
opening commercial plug. What did it warn listeners
about?

27. What crime series of the 1930s and 1940s touted itself as
offering "authentic" stories of local police and federal
G-men "at war" against the criminal underworld?

28. What crime series sternly reminded listeners every week
that "this is not an official program of the FBI"?

29. Effie Perrine was the secretary to what Dashiell Hammett
detective hero?

30. What 1940s crime series opened with footsteps, a fog-
horn, gunshots, a police whistle, and organ music, followed by the introduction of the title character as a man
who came "out of the fog, out of the night"?

ANSWERS

1. *Basil Rathbone and Nigel Bruce, who also played the characters in the series of theatrical films done at the same time.*

2. Jack Webb. *The character served him well on both radio and television versions of* Dragnet *through two decades, beginning in 1949.*

3. *Ben Romero, played by Barton Yarborough until his death in 1951. Ben Alexander replaced him in both the radio and the television versions of the series, playing the role of Frank Smith.*

4. Ellery Queen. *Not surprisingly, professional mystery writers made the best armchair detectives.*

5. The Adventures of Sam Spade.

6. Yours Truly, Johnny Dollar. *Dollar was an insurance investigator who narrated his own adventures, presenting them as explanations of his expenditures. When he had wrapped up the case (and the billing), he signed off: "Yours truly, Johnny Dollar."*

7. *Nero Wolfe. The character first appeared in a series of novels written by Rex Stout. Sydney Greenstreet was the most famous performer to assume the radio lead, playing the part during the early 1950s.*

8. *Nick and Nora Charles (and Asta). The 1941–1950 radio series faithfully duplicated the style of the successful* Thin Man *films, placing as much attention on the couple's light banter as on the murder mystery itself. Nick Charles, by the way, was not the* Thin Man. *The name referred to another character in the original theatrical film. The title stuck, though, as a hook for subsequent adventures of Nick and Nora.*

9. *Brad Runyon, better known as the Fat Man. He was a slick and*

sophisticated detective adventurer, like the hero of The Thin Man.
But unlike that series, the Fat Man *title actually did refer to the main
character.*

10. *Dick Powell. His 1949* Richard Diamond, Private Detective
*series was done with a light touch and even managed to work in an
occasional song by Powell at the end.*

11. *Simon Templar, better known as the Saint. The radio series began in the mid-1940s, following the success of the character (created by Leslie Charteris) in books, magazines, and theatrical films.
Price was the third to play the role on the radio version, but his
portrayal was one of the most effective.*

12. *Orson Welles, the same actor who played Harry Lime in the
feature film. The radio series was called* The Lives of Harry Lime.

13. *Humphrey Bogart and Lauren Bacall. They played Slate Shannon and Sailor Duval, operators of a Cuban hotel. The title referred
to Shannon's boat,* Bold Venture, *which they used in many of their
adventures in the Caribbean.*

14. Pete Kelly's Blues. *Webb played Pete Kelly, leader of Pete
Kelly's Big Seven jazz combo. He repeated the role in a 1955 theatrical film and then produced and directed, but did not act in, a 1959
television series version.*

15. *Jack Webb. He took the* Pat Novak *lead role in 1946 but left the
program after only a few months. He did virtually the same character in a short-lived summer series in 1947,* Johnny Madero, *then returned to* Pat Novak. *All of this was just warm-up, of course, for*
Dragnet, *which Webb created in 1949.*

16. *Nick Carter. Before his decade-long radio run, Carter had built
a following as a pulp magazine hero, beginning back in the late
1880s. Still, a number of other radio heroes might have questioned
the immodest radio introduction to* Nick Carter, Master Detective.

17. The FBI in Peace and War, *which aired from 1944 to 1958.*

18. *Arlene Francis.*

19. *Candy Matson, played by Natalie Masters. She was a tough but
feminine detective whose series ran from 1949 to 1951.*

20. Broadway Is My Beat. *The program played into the mid-1950s.*

21. *Boston Blackie.*

22. Crime Doctor. *The radio program was also adapted for a series of theatrical films during the 1940s.*

23. *Johnny Dollar.*

24. *Police detective Chameleon was a master of disguise.*

25. *Mr. Keen. The program was called Mr. Keen,* Tracer of Lost Persons, *and it ran from the late 1930s to the mid-1950s. Parodies by Bob and Ray on their radio programs twisted the odd-sounding title into* Mr. Trace, Keener Than Most Persons *and* Mr. Treet, Chaser of Lost People.

26. *Five o'clock shadow. As a clock chimed in the background, the announcer whispered ominously: "Avoid—five—o'clock—shadow! Use Gem Blades!"*

27. Gangbusters. *The weekly series was done with the cooperation of the FBI's J. Edgar Hoover and some local authorities. Though Hoover let the program have access only to information on cases that had been wrapped up, this still gave it a justified claim to some authenticity. Strictly speaking, though, the writers generally used this information as a jumping-off point for a chiefly fictionalized adventure, usually told from the point of view of the criminals involved. Of course, lawful authority always triumphed.*

28. The FBI in Peace and War. *The show may not have been an official presentation of the Bureau, but it always presented the agency in a very positive light.*

29. Sam Spade. Effie, *played by Lurene Tuttle, dutifully suffered through Sam's advances toward each week's beautiful client during the 1946–1951 run of* The Adventures of Sam Spade.

30. Bulldog Drummond. *The character was a British sleuth who had been featured in a number of films in the 1930s. Though the stories in the radio series were only average, the program had a strong sense of atmosphere, no doubt due to its producer-director, Himan Brown, creator of* Inner Sanctum Mysteries. *One of the more unusual aspects of Bulldog Drummond, however, was that its distinctive opening turned up again more than twenty-five years later* *as the basis for a similar sequence ("out of the fog, into the smog") in a late 1960s send-up of the radio crime genre by the Firesign Theatre comedy troupe. Their detective adventure parody was released in 1969 on the album* How Can You Be in Two Places at Once When You're Not Anywhere at All.

Adventure Heroes

1. Though the character of the Shadow had been on radio since the early 1930s, the avenging man of mystery did not become a big hit until 1937. At that time, who stepped into the leading roles of the Shadow and his confidante, Margo Lane?

2. Why did Tonto dub young John Reid the Lone Ranger?

3. What adventure series featured the direct descendant of the Lone Ranger?

4. Name the Green Hornet's faithful valet and his sleek, supercharged automobile.

5. What western hero had a young companion named Little Beaver?

6. How did ace flyer Captain Midnight get his name?

7. What 1940s adventure series featured the daredevil exploits of "America's ace of the airways"?

8. Whom did Sergeant Preston rely on for backup in his pursuit of lawbreakers in the Yukon territory?

9. What adventure serial followed the exploits of a young man from the twentieth century who fell into suspended animation and woke up five hundred years later?

10. Name the two radio adventure series of the 1930s and 1940s that were based on newspaper comic strips done by artist Milton Caniff.

11. What two western heroes rode horses named Silver and Scout?

12. Name "America's famous fighting cowboy," who brought his comic strip adventures to radio in 1942.

13. What "straight-shooting" cowboy adventure series had as its sponsor Ralston cereals of Checkerboard Square?

14. What cowboy star was host of a weekly program of stories and songs from Melody Ranch?

15. Who took the title role in the *Hopalong Cassidy* radio series, and who played his partner?

16. What role did the daughter of Edgar Rice Burroughs play in the early 1930s syndicated version of *Tarzan*?

17. Name the Lee Falk comic strip magician who appeared on radio in the early 1940s, aided by his powerful servant Lothar and the beautiful Princess Narda.

18. In a 1930s adventure series, American Frank Chandler battled the forces of evil, using mystical secrets he had learned in the Far East. By what name was he better known?

19. What Harold Gray comic strip character served as the basis for one of the first child-oriented radio adventure serials, which ran from 1931 to 1943?

20. What 1940s adventure series occasionally featured costumed crime fighters Batman and his sidekick, Robin as guest stars?

21. What early 1950s hero was touted as "Guardian of the forests! Protector of wildlife! Champion of man and nature!"?

22. In the mid-1940s, who replaced Uncle Jim as mentor to Jack Armstrong, Billy, and Betty?

23. Jack Packard, Doc Long, and Reggie Yorke were the daring heroes of what popular adventure series?

24. What action anthology of the 1940s and 1950s opened with the promise of a show "designed to free you from the four walls of today for a half-hour of high adventure"?

25. *I Love Adventure* was a 1948 summer adventure series that brought back the characters from what popular cliffhanger of a few years before?

26. What adventure series featured the schemes of the villainous Ivan Shark?

27. Name the arch foe of Buck Rogers.

28. What adventure series featured the villainous Dragon Lady?

29. What food product did Popeye the sailor man push on his 1930s radio series?

30. Young fans of Jack Armstrong were encouraged to follow a three-point training program in the early 1940s to keep in shape. The first two rules were: get lots of fresh air, sleep, and exercise; and use plenty of soap and water every day. What was rule number three?

ANSWERS

1. *Orson Welles and Agnes Moorehead. They were actually the first to play the characters that built* The Shadow's *longtime radio following. Prior to 1937, the Shadow had been used merely as an introductory narrator to some crime thriller stories. In 1937, he became the dark avenger who knew "what evil lurks in the hearts of men" and was quite willing to dispense appropriate justice himself. Welles stayed with his character until late 1938, and Moorehead continued hers a bit longer. A number of performers succeeded them, carrying the program into the 1950s.*

2. *Reid was the only survivor of six Texas Rangers caught in a deadly ambush. Members of the Butch Cavendish gang had trapped the pursuing rangers in a canyon, cut them down from a distance with high-powered rifles, and left them all for dead. John Reid, however, was still alive when Tonto came upon the site. As the Indian nursed Reid back to health, he observed, "You only Ranger left. You Lone Ranger."*

3. The Green Hornet. *Both series were created by George Trendle, who established the character of the Green Hornet as Britt Reid, son of Dan Reid, the nephew of John Reid (the Lone Ranger).*

4. *Kato was his valet, who usually drove the speedy Black Beauty.*

5. *Red Ryder.*

6. *He flew back in triumph at midnight from a near impossible mission behind enemy lines, earning the moniker Captain Midnight. The name also reinforced his image as a mysterious man of action.*

7. Hop Harrigan. *Most of Hop Harrigan's wartime adventures involved flying life-or-death missions behind enemy lines. (He always came through.) After the war, he battled conventional*

American criminals. The series ran for six years, beginning in August 1942.

8. *Yukon King, the lead dog in his sled team.*

9. Buck Rogers in the Twenty-Fifth Century.

10. Terry and the Pirates, *beginning in the late 1930s, and the syndicated* Steve Canyon, *beginning in the late 1940s. In fact, Milton Caniff's 1947* Steve Canyon *strip even received a sneak preview on NBC television in New York when the artist sketched one of the characters on camera.*

11. *The Lone Ranger and Tonto. The Ranger's nephew, Dan Reid, rode a horse named Victor.*

12. *Red Ryder, created by Fred Harmon. The newspaper strip was already an established success when the radio series began, so the red-haired cowboy did well in his new medium, even when slotted against another western hero, the Lone Ranger.*

13. The Tom Mix (Ralston) Straightshooters. *Tom even sang the praises of shredded Ralston in the opening commercial.*

14. *Gene Autry. The program was set up as a foot-stomping party "around the campfire" at Autry's western home, Melody Ranch.*

15. *William Boyd, who had played Hopalong Cassidy in more than sixty theatrical films, continued the role on radio. Andy Clyde played his partner, California.*

16. *Jane. Joan Burroughs was married to the original leading man in the radio series, James Pierce.*

17. *Mandrake the Magician.*

18. *Chandler the Magician. The original series ran from 1932 to 1936, then was revived for a two-year run beginning in 1948.*

19. *Little Orphan Annie.*

20. The Adventures of Superman. *Oddly, Batman and Robin never received their own show.*

21. *Mark Trail. The series was based on the popular comic strip and usually focused on Trail's efforts to protect the forests from human destruction.*

22. *Vic Hardy, a reformed criminal who had been one of the team's long-running foes.*

23. I Love a Mystery. *Jack was the team's level-headed leader, Doc was its fiery Texas fighter, and Reggie was its slick British partner. Together they operated the A-1 Detective Agency and traveled the world in search of adventure and mystery.*

24. Escape. *The series ran from the late 1940s to the mid-1950s and was characterized by tight writing and consistently good casting. William Conrad was a frequent performer and also handled the dramatic opening.*

25. I Love a Mystery. *Carlton Morse, writer of the original series, returned for I Love Adventure, and so did the two surviving leads, Michael Raffetto and Barton Yarborough (Walter Paterson had died). The new setting did not catch on, however, so the following year the original I Love a Mystery was restaged using the original scripts and a new cast, including Tony Randall in Paterson's role as Reggie Yorke.*

26. Captain Midnight. *Luckily, the captain and his secret squadron always managed to thwart Ivan Shark just in time.*

27. *Killer Kane. The two went at it through the entire twelve-year run of the series (1932–1936 and 1939–1947). Kane was sometimes aided by the evil villainess, Ardala Valmar.*

28. Terry and the Pirates. *The Dragon Lady matched wits with Terry Lee and his buddies throughout the decade-long run of the series.*

29. *Wheatena cereal. Although Popeye ate spinach for strength, he also plugged the body-building qualities of the sponsor's cereal.*

30. *Eat a healthful "breakfast of champions" every morning. This message was consistently hammered home by Wheaties, the program's sponsor, which billed itself as "the breakfast of champions."*

Mystery, Suspense, and Drama

1. Name the NBC horror series, created by Wyllis Cooper in 1934 and taken over by Arch Oboler in 1936, that staged some of the most frightening stories ever broadcast on radio.

2. In *Sorry, Wrong Number* Agnes Moorehead played Elbert Stevenson, an invalid unable to convince anyone she telephoned that she had overheard a murder plot through some crossed wires on her phone line. Who was the intended victim?

3. What 1940s horror anthology series began with the eerie sound of a creaking, squeaking door slowly opening?

4. Name the chilling Orson Welles science fiction tale that presented the schemes and sufferings of a severed human brain kept alive in a tank.

5. Name the director and producer of *Inner Sanctum Mysteries* who was also associated with such programs as *Adventures of the Thin Man*, *Bulldog Drummond*, and *Joyce Jordan, Girl Interne*.

6. What drama anthology presented its weekly productions from "the Little Theater off Times Square"?

7. When *The Lux Radio Theater* moved from New York City to Hollywood in 1936, what big-name film director joined the program as host and producer?

8. What big-name film stars appeared in the first Hollywood-based production of *The Lux Radio Theater*, "The Legionnaire and the Lady," on June 1, 1936?

9. Who played the title role in *The Lux Radio Theater's* adaptations of the hit films *The Jolson Story* and *Jolson Sings Again*?

10. Who played the part of Ebenezer Scrooge so effectively that he practically turned the radio production of *A Christmas Carol* into his own personal Christmas tradition, restaging the story on various programs from 1934 to the 1950s?

11. Name the writer and director of such series as *Words without Music, Passport for Adams,* and *Columbia Presents Corwin.*

12. Who played the title character in the 1943 series *Passport for Adams,* the story of a small-town newspaper editor on a goodwill mission to America's allies overseas?

13. Who originally played Steve Wilson, the tough, dedicated editor of *The Illustrated Press* on *The Big Town*?

14. What drama anthology began each presentation at a New York City train terminal and then followed particular passengers from there into that week's story?

15. What mysterious figure arrived each week on a train, ready to tell another terrifying suspense tale?

16. What mysterious figure was the narrator of suspense stories with a twist, introducing himself at the beginning of each episode with this line: "I know many things, for I walk by night"?

17. Name the 1947 NBC mystery anthology series featuring Peter Lorre playing a variety of characters "on the edge."

18. What scary mystery anthology—aimed at kids—featured Roger Elliott, the Mystery Man as narrator?

19. Old Nancy (accompanied by her black cat, Satan) was narrator of one of the first major horror series of the 1930s. What was the show?

20. Name the drama anthology series that was presented by Father Patrick Peyton of the Holy Cross Fathers and that focused for ten years on the value of the family and prayer.

21. Name the late 1940s series, based on a book by Fulton Oursler, that dramatized the life of Jesus Christ.

22. *The Screen Guild Theater* premiered in 1939 and quickly attracted some of the most famous Hollywood performers. What was the standard fee paid to the big-name stars who appeared on the program?

23. What prestigious drama anthology series recreated events in American history and literature, with subjects ranging from young Abe Lincoln to Babe Ruth?

24. In the summer of 1937, CBS and NBC offered competing adaptations of Shakespeare's plays on Monday nights. Who was the producer, adaptor, and occasional star of NBC's entry, *Streamlined Shakespeare*?

25. Name the western anthology series created by Ruth Woodman and sponsored by the Pacific Coast Borax Company.

ANSWERS

1. Lights Out. *The series opened with the chilling sound of the twelve chimes of midnight, signaling the start of "the witching hour." For maximum effect, the program's announcer urged members of the home audience to "turn out your lights." The stories made quite an impression, especially on young listeners. In the mid-1960s, comedian Bill Cosby, who had grown up with the series, described being frightened by the* Lights Out *presentation of "Chicken Heart." Cosby's lengthy routine included his running narration of the story, complete with sound effects, including the incessant "thumpa-thumpa" of the Chicken Heart "in search of human blood." The entire skit was included on Cosby's 1966 album* Wonderfulness, *a tribute to the inventiveness and effectiveness of* Lights Out.

2. *She was. Initially Stevenson did not realize that she was the target of the plot, so instead of leaving her house to seek safety she spent her time trying to get help for an unidentified person. These efforts were stymied by the fact that she could not provide the name or location of the intended victim. Even if they believed her, police and other authorities had to dismiss her calls because there was no indication of where they should go. By the time Elbert Stevenson figured out what was going on, she was too late to save herself.*

3. Inner Sanctum Mysteries. *Of course, the program closed with the door creaking shut.*

4. *"Donovan's Brain." The story played as a two-part presentation on the* Suspense *drama anthology during the 1940s.*

5. *Himan Brown.*

6. The First Nighter Program, *which began in 1930. Of course, there was no such place as "the Little Theater off Times Square," but the program created the illusion of attending an opening night* *performance on Broadway—right down to sound effects of bustling Manhattan traffic, attentive ushers, and a packed house.*

7. *Cecil B. De Mille. He brought with him the image of larger-than-life big-budget Hollywood production, which was just what the program needed to boost its shaky ratings. It worked.*

8. *Clark Gable and Marlene Dietrich. Small wonder that the program's talent budget easily passed $10,000 each week.*

9. *Al Jolson himself. In the 1946 and 1949 theatrical films, Larry Parks played the part of Jolson.*

10. *Lionel Barrymore. He even incorporated it into his own regular weekly series from 1942 to 1949.*

11. *Norman Corwin. He had a flair for light verse and used it on such productions as his 1938 tale of the devil's "Plot to Overthrow Christmas." Corwin also drew on the works of poets such as Walt Whitman, Carl Sandburg, and Edgar Lee Masters for some dramatizations. He worked chiefly for CBS on various shows from the late 1930s into the 1950s.*

12. *Robert Young. He played Jeff Adams, an editor who traveled to various Allied countries gathering firsthand information on the war effort to send back to the folks at home. The series was written by CBS drama veteran Norman Corwin, who had worked on a government propaganda series,* This Is War, *the previous year.*

13. *Edward G. Robinson. He stayed with the character from the 1937 premiere until 1942. The series ran another ten years after his departure.*

14. Grand Central Station.

15. *The Mysterious Traveler. He acted as narrator of the series but never participated in the stories.* The Mysterious Traveler *ran from the early 1940s to the early 1950s.*

16. *The Whistler. The program opened with the sound of his footsteps and, of course, his distinctive whistle.*

17. Mystery in the Air. *The anthology program specialized in classic crime stories and characters such as Jack the Ripper.*

18. The House of Mystery. *John Griggs played Roger Elliott, who was supposed to be an expert ghost chaser.*

19. The Witch's Tale. *A sensible title, after all, because Old Nancy was introduced as a witch from Salem.*

20. Family Theater. *The program was not a formally religious show. It just embraced a definite point of view about the value of families, running with that from 1947 to 1957.*

21. The Greatest Story Ever Told. *The show began in 1947 as a Sunday offering on ABC and was widely praised for handling the subject with style and good taste.*

22. Nothing. *All of the stars' fees were donated by the sponsor, Gulf Oil, to the Motion Picture Relief Fund. Within just a few years, Gulf had put nearly a million dollars toward this cause.*

23. Cavalcade of America. *The program ran from the mid-1930s to the early 1950s.*

24. *John Barrymore.* Streamlined Shakespeare *certainly lived up to its name, compressing each presentation into forty-five minutes— plenty of time for the famous bits and some transitional narration.*

25. Death Valley Days. *The program, which ran from 1930 to 1945, presented stories set in the Old West of the 1870s. In 1945, the series changed its format and became* Death Valley Days Sheriff, *featuring a modern-day cowboy detective.*

Soap Operas

1. Why were the daytime serials aimed at housewives dubbed soap operas?

2. Name the 1943 Erle Stanley Gardner soap operalike crime series that ran on weekday afternoons on CBS for more than a decade.

3. What soap opera mother lost her son John as a casualty in World War II?

4. Who was the creator of such soaps as *The Guiding Light*, *The Right to Happiness*, *Today's Children*, and *Road of Life*?

5. What creative team was responsible for such soaps as *Backstage Wife*, *Just Plain Bill*, *Lorenzo Jones*, and *Stella Dallas*?

6. Who was the creator and writer of such soap operas as *Pepper Young's Family*, *When a Girl Marries*, and *Rosemary*?

7. The first soap opera created by Irna Phillips in 1930 focused on the Moynihan family and began its suds on Chicago's WGN. Name the series.

8. What soap was affectionately known to its ardent fans as "Elsie Beebe"?

9. What epic soap opera presented the story of the Barbour family of Sea Cliff, San Francisco?

10. When *The Story of Dr. Kildare* began its soapy syndicated run in 1949, who stepped into the leading roles of Dr. James Kildare and Dr. Leonard Gillespie?

11. What afternoon soap opera on NBC was played as a light comedy, focusing on the antics of a tinkering mechanic and part-time inventor at Jim Barker's garage?

12. What soap opera had as its simple opening theme a piano rendition of Debussy's "Clair de Lune"?

13. Four chimes from the clock in the Glen Falls Town Hall signaled the beginning of what long-running soap opera?

14. Name the soap opera that followed a young woman raising her two children, Janie and Mark, after the death of her husband, torn between what she owed them and what she owed herself.

15. Who played the leading role of Mother Moran during the 1930s run of the soap opera *Today's Children*?

16. What self-sacrificing soap mother of the late 1930s "saw her own beloved daughter Laurel marry into wealth and society, and, realizing the differences in their tastes and worlds, went out of Laurel's life"?

17. What soap presented the struggles of a career woman who was set up to prove that "because a woman is thirty-five, and more, romance in life need not be over; that the romance of youth can extend into middle life, and even beyond"?

18. What low-key soap opera of the early 1930s was named for its three gossipy apartment house neighbors?

19. What soap presented the homespun philosophies of Bill Davidson, a barber in the town of Hartville?

20. What long-running NBC soap opera followed the trials and tribulations of the Young family in the middle-American town of Elmwood?

21. What soap opera featured an orphan who married a British lord, only to face the question, "can this girl from a mining town in the West find happiness as the wife of a wealthy and titled Englishman?"?

22. What soap opera began its run in 1932 with Elizabeth Reller as a young woman of humble background and Don Ameche as a rich young man who gave up his family fortune to marry her?

23. What soap opera presented the quiet struggles of Mary Noble, a sweet young girl from Iowa who married Broadway's most handsome leading man, Larry Noble?

24. Name the soap that told the story of Joan Barrett and her increasingly unstable husband, Dr. Truman Scott.

25. Name the soap opera that began in 1940 and presented Lucille Wall as a brilliant attorney raising her young son, Dickie, alone following the death of her crusading husband.

26. What soap opera focused for its first seven years on the Reverend John Ruthledge, a minister in the town of Five Points?

27. In the early 1940s, the soapy *Dr. Christian* program turned to an unusual source for scripts. What was it?

28. Who played Dr. Christian on radio and in the series of spin-off theatrical films?

29. What award-winning 1939 soap opera was set in a small U.S. college town and focused on the developing world war situation as viewed by professor Jason Allen and his family?

30. What 1944 soap opera revived a previous series, *We Love and Learn,* shifting the action to Harlem and using an all-black cast?

31. In 1939, the Kransky family from *The Guilding Light* moved over to a new soap opera. What was the spin-off show?

32. When Irna Phillips began her *Woman in White* soap opera in 1938, she used the cast of another of her popular

programs to help introduce the new show. Name that other series.

33. What soap opera beginning in 1939 presented the story of Joan and Harry Davis in a program touted as "a tender, human story of young married life, dedicated to everyone who has ever been in love"?

34. What soap began in 1944 with Betty Winkler in the title role of a young secretary living with her mom and her sister Patti?

35. What soap opera followed the adventures of young Carol "Chichi" Conrad, adopted daughter of Papa David Solomon, owner of the Slightly Read Bookshop?

36. What soap opera of the 1930s and 1940s followed the show business careers of two young women who started together as "kids in the chorus" on Broadway back in 1931?

37. In what soap opera did the main character take over her husband's job as U.S. senator from Iowa when he disappeared in 1939 during an overseas diplomatic mission?

38. What soap opera's leading character had as his grand dream heading the Three Oaks Medical Clinic?

39. On the final episode of *Young Widder Brown* in 1956, whom did Ellen Brown agree to marry?

40. On November 25, 1960, CBS ended the era of radio soap operas. What four stalwarts were there at the very end?

ANSWERS

1. *Many were sponsored by producers of various soap products. The name stuck, along with others such as "sudsers" and simply "soaps."*

2. Perry Mason. *In contrast to Raymond Burr's level-headed portrayal of the character on television in the 1950s and 1960s, radio's Perry Mason was far more short-tempered and irresponsible. He still won his cases, but with plenty of soapy complications along the way.*

3. *Ma Perkins. When the character of John was killed off in 1944, the program was swamped with letters. The decision to let him die in the war was defended, though, as a realistic plot development. After all, many real-life mothers had lost sons to the war and so why not Ma Perkins?*

4. *Irna Phillips. She was one of the most successful and prolific soap opera writers on radio. During her heyday in the 1940s, she reportedly turned out millions of words of script annually.*

5. *Frank and Anne Hummert. They supervised the programs from beginning to end through their own production company, using a team of writers to flesh out their plot outlines.*

6. *Elaine Carrington. She dictated the scripts to her secretary and also handled the rewriting and editing. Though she did not have as many series as her competitors, Frank and Anne Hummert and Irna Phillips, each of her three top programs ran for more than ten years.*

7. Painted Dreams. *When Irna Phillips split with WGN, she used the same basic hooks for a successful soap on NBC,* Today's Children, *which ran from 1933 to 1938 and from 1943 to 1950. WGN's version of* Painted Dreams, *without any help from Phillips, had only a brief network run (1933–1934) on CBS.*

8. Life Can Be Beautiful, *which ran from 1938 to 1954. The nickname came from the first letter in each word of the title:* L.C.B.B. *(Elsie Beebe).*

9. One Man's Family. *The program ran for twenty-seven years, beginning in 1932, and followed the Barbour family through three generations.*

10. *Lew Ayres and Lionel Barrymore, who had played the parts in a series of theatrical films featuring the characters during the 1930s and 1940s. Their relationship followed the quintessential medical drama setup: the young idealistic surgeon and his crusty but lovable older mentor.*

11. Lorenzo Jones. *Karl Swenson played the title character as a lovable, if impractical, dreamer. Belle, his loving wife, stood by to help, no matter how silly his latest scheme turned out to be.*

12. The Story of Mary Marlin, *which ran on network radio from 1935 to 1945 and then from 1951 to 1952.*

13. Big Sister, *which began in 1936 and played until 1952.*

14. Young Widder Brown.

15. *Irna Phillips. She had patterned the character after her own mother and so, appropriately, decided to play the part herself. She dropped the character (and the series, for a while) in 1938 following the death of her mother.*

16. Stella Dallas. *Of course, despite her apprehensions about her lack of formal education, Stella did not really get out of Laurel's life. Nonetheless, Stella had some exciting adventures on her own, including run-ins with thieves, international travel, and murder investigations. Not bad for a Boston seamstress. The program ran until 1955.*

17. The Romance of Helen Trent. *She carried on her romantic adventures from 1933 to the spring of 1960.*

18. Clara, Lu and Em. *The characters evolved out of routines done by the original leads (Louise Starkey, Isabel Carothers, and Helen King) when they attended Northwestern University during the 1920s.*

19. Just Plain Bill, *which ran from 1932 to 1955.*

20. Pepper Young's Family. *The program ran from 1936 to 1959, focusing on the simple complications in their everyday lives. Pepper was the family's hardworking son who, during the course of the series, even married his childhood sweetheart, Linda.*

21. Our Gal Sunday, *which ran from 1937 to 1959. The main character was named Sunday by the miners who raised her in the town of Silver Creek, Colorado.*

22. Betty and Bob. *A succession of performers followed in both roles over the years, carrying on the soapy tribulations. This was the first daytime soap opera from Frank and Anne Hummert.*

23. Backstage Wife. *Mary certainly had her hands full over the twenty-three-year run of the series (beginning in 1935). After all, it was not easy being married to "the dream sweetheart of a million other women."*

24. Valiant Lady. *True to the title, Joan not only gave up her acting career to be a homemaker, but also had to work hard to keep Truman's feet "planted firmly upon the pathway to success."*

25. Portia Faces Life.

26. The Guilding Light. *When the minister went to war, the other characters assumed more importance in the Five Points setting. By the end of the 1940s, the Ruthledge character had been phased out.*

27. *The home audience. The program solicited scripts from listeners, awarding monetary prizes for the best ones and paying less for others used on the series. During this period, the program became a listener-written anthology series essentially focusing on one main character, Dr. Christian.*

28. *Jean Hersholt, who created the character. The program ran on CBS radio from the late 1930s to the early 1950s.*

29. Against the Storm. *The program was one of the first to deal exclusively with the effects and implications of the war in Europe, two years before the United States entered the conflict. Because the show was set at a college, there was the opportunity to work in philosophical war discussions—and even to have guest lecturers such as poet Edgar Lee Masters.*

30. The Story of Ruby Valentine. *Juanita Hall played the title role.*

31. The Right to Happiness. *Ironically, these characters were soon overshadowed by the restless "search for happiness" by the character Carolyn Allen Walker Kramer Nelson McDonald, who went through four husbands over the course of the series.*

32. Today's Children. Woman in White *was actually a replacement for that series after Irna Phillips chose to suspend production on* Today's Children. *When the program returned in late 1943, its characters' lives once again intertwined with those of the* Woman in White *characters.*

33. When a Girl Marries.

34. Rosemary.

35. Life Can Be Beautiful. *Under Solomon's affectionate eye, Carol grew into young adulthood as an attractive, popular woman.*

36. Myrt and Marge.

37. The Story of Mary Marlin. *Actually, he was alive but had amnesia (of course). Eventually he returned to the States.*

38. Young Dr. Malone. *The saga of Jerry Malone, a young doctor living in Three Oaks, began in 1939. By the end of its run, twenty-one years later, Dr. Malone had achieved his dream.*

39. *Dr. Anthony Loring, her longtime suitor.*

40. Ma Perkins *(on since August 1933),* The Right to Happiness *(on since October 1939),* Young Dr. Malone *(on since November 1939), and* The Second Mrs. Burton *(on since January 1946).*

Games and Quizzes

1. *Take It or Leave It* was better known by the dollar value of the final question contestants had to answer to win the program's top prize. What was it?

2. Name the announcer on *You Bet Your Life.*

3. Who was host of *Truth or Consequences* through its entire 1940–1957 radio run?

4. Name the series hosted by Arlene Francis in which six men competed for dates with three women hidden on the other side of a studio screen.

5. Who was the "mental banker" who offered silver dollars as prizes on the spot to members of the studio audience who could answer his questions?

6. What 1930s musical quizmaster used the line, "That's wrong, you're right"?

7. Name the radio quiz show created by Louis G. Cowan in 1940 as an entertaining showcase for a panel of brilliant children.

8. What humorous stunt show sent one of its weekly contestants out into the real world to perform some silly task and then report back to the studio by the end of the program?

9. Who was the energetic host of *Stop the Music*?

10. Who was the host of *House Party,* both on radio and during its daytime television run?

11. Who was the original host of *People Are Funny*?

12. Who was the adult quizmaster to the panel of child geniuses on *The Quiz Kids*?

13. Who was the host and creator of the 1940s show, *Juvenile Jury*?

14. What quiz series featured a resident panel of experts challenged each week by moderator Clifton Fadiman to answer questions sent in by the home audience?

15. What series featured Albert Mitchell with answers to straightforward questions from listeners such as "Was there snow on the first Thanksgiving?"?

16. Name the humorous quiz show that set itself up as the reverse of such fact-filled series as *Information Please,* presenting silly answers to such simple questions as "Who is buried in Grant's Tomb"?

17. Who were the three panelists and the host on *It Pays to Be Ignorant*?

18. Harry Hershfield, Joe Laurie, Jr., and "Senator" Ed Ford formed the joke-judging panel for what popular game show of the 1940s?

19. The 1948 series *Life Begins at 80* featured freewheeling discussion from a panel of octogenarians—in a simple reversal of what popular juvenile show?

20. What was the function of the "guest male" on the humorous advice program, *Leave It to the Girls*?

21. How did listeners at home win money on *Stop the Music*?

22. Starting in 1939, a giveaway show called *Pot o' Gold* began calling listeners at home and awarding them cash prizes (as much as $1,000). What did they have to do to win?

23. On CBS's 1943–1953 game show, *Grand Slam,* how did the contestants score a "grand slam"?

24. What quiz program on ABC dethroned two of radio's comedy superstars within ten months of its premiere in March 1948?

25. What game show used "Beulah the buzzer" to indicate that contestants had failed to answer correctly the question put to them?

26. Name the creator of *You Bet Your Life, House Party,* and *People Are Funny.*

27. Why did *You Bet Your Life* record nearly an hour of material for each show, yet use only about half of it?

28. In the mid-1940s, *Truth or Consequences* added an occasional running contest to guess the identity of a celebrity hidden offstage. Who was the star identified in 1946 as Mrs. Hush?

ANSWERS

1. *The $64 question. The contest was set up as a series of increasingly difficult questions in a specific category, with the dollar value doubling at each stage (beginning with $1 and ending with $64). With each correct answer, contestants would move on to the next level. One incorrect answer, though, and they would lose everything. Thus, the $64 final question became the trademark of the show. When the program moved to television in the 1950s, the payoff jumped from $64 to $64,000.*

2. *George Fenneman, who played straight man to Groucho Marx.*

3. *Ralph Edwards.*

4. Blind Date. *Three of the men would win dates, usually consisting of an evening at a New York nightclub.*

5. *Dr. I.Q. Members of the Dr. I.Q. program staff would go into the audience with microphones, find contestants, and then have Dr. I.Q. ask his question. If the contestants answered correctly, the "mental banker" paid off in silver dollars.*

6. *Kay Kyser. On his* College of Musical Knowledge, *Kyser would sometimes tell contestants to answer a question in reverse—that is, if the answer was "True," they should say "False." Thus, they were "right" when they were "wrong." If they slipped and gave the correct answer, they lost because then they were "wrong" because they had been "right," leading Kyser to say, "That's right, you're wrong!"*

7. The Quiz Kids. *The program was an all-around information game show that featured a panel of children facing questions submitted by listeners. Though a number of children stayed on the show for years, there were always guest spots available to make room for some new pre-teen genius.*

8. People Are Funny. *While these contestants were "on assignment," others were put through the paces in the studio. Naturally, someone from the show went along outside to keep an eye on those players so that they did not tell the passersby what was really going on. Instead, the contestants dutifully had to perform their tasks, such as the surprisingly difficult job of giving away money to total strangers, and then come back to the studio by the end of the program and report on the results.*

9. *Bert Parks.*

10. *Art Linkletter.*

11. *Art Baker, who ran the program from its premiere in 1942 until October 1943. Then he was replaced by Art Linkletter who had been his co-host for a few episodes at the beginning of the series.*

12. *Joe Kelly. Ironically, he was a grammar school dropout and had previously been part of the good-time music on* The National Barn Dance *rather than a quizmaster. Yet he managed to mesh well with the children, perhaps because on the air he did not hide the fact that the abilities of the quiz kids often floored him (just as they no doubt floored the audience at home). He also did not try to compete with them, instead focusing his energy on keeping the show moving along in an entertaining manner.*

13. *Jack Barry.*

14. Information Please. *Listeners received a prize if their questions were used—and a bigger prize if they stumped the panel. The program also included guest celebrity panelists such as Fred Allen, Gracie Allen, and Alfred Hitchcock.*

15. The Answer Man. *Unlike celebrity-oriented informational programs that used questions as a springboard for clever repartee, this series generally stuck to providing the answers. The Answer Man ran from the late 1930s to the early 1950s in syndication, receiving thousands of questions each week from listeners.*

16. It Pays to Be Ignorant. *The program emphasized the comic responses of its three panelists when faced with absurdly easy questions, so contestants won cash essentially for just standing there feeding the panel straight lines.*

17. *George Shelton, Harry McNaughton, Lulu McConnell, and host Tom Howard. All four performed well as quiz show participants who were far more interested in getting a good laugh than in answering the questions. Shelton and Howard were buddies from vaudeville while McNaughton and McConnell had cut their teeth in Broadway revues and musicals.*

18. Can You Top This? *The premise of the program was simple. Host Peter Donald would read jokes selected from the hundreds submitted each week by listeners at home. Each panelist would attempt to top these jokes, and a large "laugh gauge" on stage would measure studio audience reaction. Listeners would receive a prize if their jokes were used—and a larger prize if the panelists were unable to come up with toppers.*

19. Juvenile Jury. *On that show, a panel of young children discussed problems and questions about kids put to them by listeners at home. On Life Begins at 80, the panelists (all eighty or older) tackled a wider range of subjects.*

20. *He was there to "defend" the male point of view. This was set up in humorous contrast to the advice offered by the panel of women responding to listeners' questions. Their comments ranged from serious to frivolous, so the men could jump in from any direction.*

21. *Listeners were called at home and asked to identify the song that had just been played on the program. If they were correct, they won a cash prize and got a chance to identify a much more difficult "mystery melody" worth as much as $30,000. Though the odds against being called were tremendous (phone numbers from across the nation were selected at random), the program immediately attracted a huge audience that wanted to be ready to win. The contestant had to be listening before being called because once he or she picked up the phone, the host would say, "Stop the music!" and the song would stop playing.*

22. *Have a telephone. The program was a mixture of music and giveaway, with most of the show devoted to musical performances. Several times during each broadcast, though, a phone number from somewhere in the United States was selected and called. If someone was at home and answered the telephone, he or she would win $1,000 just for picking up the phone (the winner did not even* *have to be listening to the show). Those who failed to answer won a small consolation cash prize. The program was a big hit in 1939 and lasted for three seasons.*

23. *By answering all five questions put to them. The sets of questions were sent in by listeners who won the prize if the studio contestants answered incorrectly.*

24. Stop the Music, *with Bert Parks. ABC and Parks had already tasted success with a flashy giveaway quiz show called* Break the Bank *in 1946. On March 21, 1948, the one-hour* Stop the Music *premiered in one of the toughest time slots on radio: Sundays from 8:00 to 9:00 P.M., opposite NBC's top-ten stars Edgar Bergen (8:00 to 8:30) and Fred Allen (8:30 to 9:00). By August, Fred Allen had dropped to thirty-eighth place in the ratings and, in the fall, even offered "insurance" to listeners who missed out on any prize money by listening to him rather than to* Stop the Music. *In December, Edgar Bergen announced that he was taking a "leave of absence" from radio for nine months.*

25. Truth or Consequences. *Following the buzzer came, of course, "the consequences."*

26. *John Guedel.*

27. *The program was set up as a showcase for the ad lib wit of Groucho Marx and consequently did not follow the same sort of formal pacing as a standard variety show or even another quiz or game show. The focus instead was on the interaction between the contestants and Marx. The longer time allowed him to go off on many humorous tangents knowing that unsuccessful or risqué sequences would be safely edited out.*

28. *Clara Bow. Others included Jack Dempsey as Mr. Hush and Jack Benny as The Walking Man.*

Golden Review

1. Throughout World War II, what popular comic rarely did his weekly variety show from the studio, performing instead at military bases and service hospitals throughout the country?

2. How did Ozzie and Harriet Nelson celebrate their ninth wedding anniversary on October 8, 1944?

3. What radio superstar defected from NBC in the fall of 1946 because he wanted to prerecord his show?

4. When William Paley led a talent raid on NBC's comedy roster in 1948, who were the first performers to ride "Paley's comet" to CBS?

5. What quiz program offered a bonus prize for inadvertently saying a "secret word"?

6. What sharp-tongued comedian carried on a running feud with Charlie McCarthy in the opening months of *The Chase and Sanborn Hour*?

7. Who played the gossipy Aunt Fanny on *The Breakfast Club*?

8. Who was known as the "bad boy of radio" in the 1940s, having earned a reputation for mercilessly mocking his sponsors and their products?

9. What CBS daytime program included an interview feature with "kids who say the darndest things"?

10. Though he was the host of successful children's shows for more than twenty years, New York's "Uncle Don" Carey received his greatest notoriety as a result of a reported event that never actually took place. What was it?

11. On December 12, 1937, Mae West incensed some listeners with her performance in a comedy skit parodying a famous scene from the Bible. What was it?

12. What unusual hook was used in the 1940s soap opera *The Light of the World* ?

13. Name the controversial radio preacher known as "the fighting priest," who delivered powerful weekly sermons to the nation throughout the 1930s.

14. Name the newspaper cartoonist who brought his eye for real-life oddities to radio throughout the 1930s and 1940s.

15. What sponsor received a sly plug with 1940s quizmaster Bob Hawk's special "Lemac" questions?

16. Who was the boy who "lived in a shoe"?

17. What 1940s children's fantasy series opened each episode by singing the praises of Cream of Wheat hot cereal?

18. Name the 1940s children's program that presented the adventures of Isabel, her brother Billy, and their friend Red Lantern (a talking fish) in a magical undersea kingdom where all the lost objects of the earth came to rest.

19. Who supplied the voice for Goo-Goo, Joe Penner's infamous duck?

20. Name the successful homespun comedy series created in 1932 by Paul Rhymer and starring Art Van Harvey and Bernardine Flynn as the Gooks family.

21. Who played the mayor of the small rural town of Springdale in *The Mayor of the Town*?

22. *The Johnson Family,* a 1930s series, first spotlighted the talents of Jimmy Scribner while presenting the story of a black family in a small southern village. What was so amazing about his characterizations?

23. Who was known as the Arkansas Traveler?

24. Name the late 1940s program hosted by Tom Bartlett, which brought real-life travelers into the studio to tell their personal tales of love, describe their home life, and explain why they were on the road.

25. Who was the host of *America's Town Meeting of the Air,* a spirited weekly debate program that specialized in placing philosophical opposites on the same stage?

26. What series featured the reviews, interviews, and critical comments of Alexander Woollcott?

27. Name the woman (once known as Martha Deane) who was the hostess of a daytime interview and light chat show from the late 1930s into the 1950s.

28. Name the program that brought to the studio a wide range of unusual hobbyists who demonstrated their interests for host Dave Elman.

29. Who was the host of *Breakfast at Sardi's* (later *Breakfast in Hollywood*), a pleasant morning program made up of light chat and good-natured fun with patrons eating breakfast at a well-known restaurant?

30. What comedy-variety show had in its family of supporting characters Walter Tetley as wise guy Julius Abbruzio, Elliott Lewis as musician Frankie Remley, and Gale Gordon as the frustrated representative of the program's sponsor, the Rexall Drug Company?

31. What show did Phil Harris spin off from?

32. Who was the announcer and expansive sports storyteller for the *Colgate Sports Newsreel,* a fifteen-minute series that ran from the late 1930s into the 1950s?

33. What popular series of MGM theatrical films had a run in the early 1950s as a syndicated radio show starring Mickey Rooney, Lewis Stone, and Fay Holden?

34. What premiere "adult western" began its radio run on CBS in April 1952?

35. Who greeted his listeners with the opening line, "Good evening, anybody"?

36. What long-running morning series used as its closing line, "Be good to yourself"?

37. Who was the creator of *Leave It to the Girls* and *Meet the Press?*

38. Who was the best-known narrator of the rapid-fire news-reel-style radio documentary series, *The March of Time?*

39. On what type of program did Hedda Hopper, Louella Parsons, and Jimmy Fidler each serve as host?

40. As part of the weekly opening sequence to the late 1940s detective series *The Fat Man,* the main character walked into a drugstore. What did he do there?

ANSWERS

1. *Bob Hope. He also made frequent trips overseas to entertain troops stationed there, a routine that he continued long after the end of World War II.*

2. *With the premiere broadcast of their own network radio show,* The Adventures of Ozzie and Harriet.

3. *Bing Crosby. The networks had a flat ban on prerecorded programs, feeling that the live nature of broadcasting was the chief asset distinguishing them from the local program syndicators. Crosby wanted to lighten his cramped schedule by prerecording his weekly* Kraft Music Hall *series at his convenience, but NBC refused. Crosby left NBC and signed with ABC as host of* Philco Radio Time, *which the network let him prerecord. With the ice broken, many other stars began prerecording their shows in the late 1940s.*

4. *Freeman Gosden and Charles Correll, who brought their* Amos and Andy *characters to CBS. William Paley used a clever tax strategy as a lure, with Gosden and Correll selling CBS the rights to the characters on their show for about $2 million.*

5. You Bet Your Life. *If a contestant just happened to use the secret word in the course of a conversation with host Groucho Marx, he or she would win a small cash prize on the spot.*

6. *W. C. Fields.*

7. *Fran Allison. She later became the middle name on the long-running children's television series,* Kukla, Fran and Ollie.

8. *Henry Morgan. He made fun not only of his sponsors (for as long as they stuck around), but also of programming executives, political institutions, businesses, and bureaucrats.*

9. House Party. *The spontaneous comments by the young children* *in the audience were one of the highlights of the program. They also served as the basis for a number of books by Art Linkletter, beginning with the title* Kids Say the Darndest Things.

10. *Supposedly at the end of one show, thinking that the mike was off, Uncle Don muttered, "I guess that'll hold the little bastards for another night." The story quickly became part of radio folklore, though Don Carey insisted that it never happened. It probably never did. But it certainly does make a great story.*

11. *The story of Adam and Eve. The sketch was written by Arch Oboler and presented on Edgar Bergen and Charlie McCarthy's show. In it, Mae West played Eve's seduction of Adam with her characteristically sensual moans, groans, and double entendres. She set off a storm of outraged protest and, in response, NBC banned her and even forbade the mention of her name on the air for years.*

12. *The soapy stories were based on characters and events taken from the Bible. Of course, the text was modernized and adapted to the soap structure, but otherwise the basics were all there, from Adam and Eve onward. Surprisingly, the program did not cause a fuss and instead ran on NBC for ten years.*

13. *Father Charles E. Coughlin. Though he remained on the air until his retirement in 1942, he reached the peak of his influence in the 1930s.*

14. *Robert Ripley. His newspaper feature,* Believe It or Not, *had built a large following for such odd items, so he brought a built-in audience to radio. The program appeared both on its own and as a segment on other series beginning in 1930, with Ripley acting as host until his death in May 1949.*

15. *Camel cigarettes. "Lemac" spelled backwards was, of course, "Camel." Hawk introduced this gimmick in the mid-1940s on his own* Bob Hawk Show.

16. *Buster Brown. The character was the identifying symbol of Buster Brown shoes and appeared inside each pair (along with his dog, Tige). On radio, he was best known as part of Smilin' Ed McConnell's children's show, usually known as* Smilin' Ed McConnell's Buster Brown Gang.

17. Let's Pretend, *sponsored by Cream of Wheat for about ten years, beginning in 1943. (Prior to that it was a sustaining show.) The program usually featured half-hour radio adaptations of traditional fairy tale favorites such as "Rumpelstiltskin" and "Sleeping Beauty." There was also an enthusiastic studio audience to cheer host Bill Adams when he invited them to come along to the magical world of Let's Pretend.*

18. Land of the Lost. *Thanks to some magic seaweed, Isabel and Billy were able to breathe underwater. Isabel Manning Hewson narrated the adventures, presenting the stories as memories of her own childhood. The series ran on Saturdays beginning in 1943 and ending in 1948.*

19. *Mel Blanc.*

20. Vic and Sade, *which ran until the mid-1940s.*

21. *Lionel Barrymore. The series ran from 1942 to 1949.*

22. *Scribner did all of the characters' voices himself. Over the years, this cast of characters grew to as many as twenty-two different roles, and the show included back-and-forth discussions and interactions. Scribner also wrote the series.*

23. *Bob Burns. He played a rural song picker and comic storyteller beginning in the mid-1930s, when he became known as the Arkansas Traveler. His Arkansas Traveler series began in 1941.*

24. Welcome, Travelers.

25. *George Denny. He not only served as moderator, but also chose the guests, with an eye toward getting a lively, timely exchange on that week's topic. The program ran from 1935 to 1956.*

26. The Town Crier. *To the cry of "Hear ye, hear ye!" Woollcott would present his opinions on the latest literary offerings. Though he was already a respected reviewer before his radio program began, once it started rolling on CBS in 1933 he quickly became one of the most influential critics in the country.*

27. *Mary Margaret McBride. She used the Martha Deane pseudonym in the very early days of her radio career.*

28. Hobby Lobby. *The program ran from the late 1930s to the late 1940s and also had a run as a television series.*

29. *Tom Breneman. When the program first appeared on network radio in 1941, it was set at Sardi's restaurant, but as it grew more popular Breneman moved the show to his own restaurant.*

30. The Phil Harris–Alice Faye Show. *The program began in 1948 when Phil Harris teamed up with his wife Alice Faye.*

31. The Jack Benny Program. *In fact, when Phil Harris (Benny's bandleader) and his wife Alice Faye first started their own charac-ter comedy as part of* The Fitch Bandwagon *show, they immediately followed Jack Benny's program. Appropriately, they used the same "show within a show" hook for their program, even referring to Phil's job with Benny, and wisely relied in the same way on a good crew of supporting characters.*

32. *Bill Stern.*

33. *The Andy Hardy films. Radio's* Hardy Family *program used the original film cast, with Mickey Rooney as Andy Hardy, Lewis Stone as his father, and Fay Holden as his mother, in what was described as the presentation of "the common joys and tribulations of the aver-age American family."*

34. Gunsmoke. *The series ran until 1961.*

35. *Henry Morgan.*

36. The Breakfast Club.

37. *Martha Rountree. She was a free-lance writer before setting up the shows.*

38. *Westbrook Van Voorhis.*

39. *A gossip program, usually focusing on show business celebri-ties.*

40. *Weigh himself. He tipped the scales at 239 pounds, so the audi-ence had no doubt that he was truly "the fat man."*

ONE-LINERS

One-Liners

Name the personalities or characters associated with each of the following phrases:

1. "Yoo-hoo! Mrs. Bloom!"
2. "Wanna buy a duck?"
3. "Coming, Mother!"
4. "What a revoltin' development this is!"
5. "Well!"
6. "S-o-o-!"
7. "Heigh-ho, everybody."
8. "I dood it!"
9. "I'm a baaad boy!"
10. "Dat's my boy dat said dat!"
11. "Around and around she goes, and where she stops nobody knows."
12. "Up, up, and away!"
13. "That's a joke, son."

ANSWERS

1. *Gertrude Berg as Molly Goldberg* on The Goldbergs.
2. *Joe Penner.*
3. *Henry Aldrich* on The Aldrich Family.
4. *William Bendix as Chester A. Riley* on The Life of Riley.
5. *Jack Benny.*
6. *Ed Wynn.*
7. *Rudy Vallee.*
8. *Red Skelton as the Mean Widdle Kid.*
9. *Lou Costello.*
10. *Jimmy Durante.*
11. *Major Edward Bowes on his* Original Amateur Hour.
12. *Superman.*
13. *Kenny Delmar as Senator Beauregard Claghorn* on The Fred Allen Show.

THE VINYL AGE
   Rock 'n' Roll
      Radio
   Radio TV
Vinyl Review

Rock 'n' Roll Radio

1. What radio sit-com performer of the early 1950s became a pop singing star with such top ten hit records as "Poor Little Fool," "For You," and "Garden Party"?

2. Name the 1956 top ten record by Buchanan and Goodman that used brief excerpts from other popular records to break in to a mock radio broadcast about an alien invasion of the earth.

3. Alan Freed, the disc jockey generally credited with popularizing rock 'n' roll music, came to New York City in the fall of 1954. What station did he join?

4. Why did Alan Freed change radio stations in 1958?

5. What drove Alan Freed off the air in New York in the late 1950s?

6. Name the comic who satirized top forty radio shows in his routines about a station known as Wonderful WINO.

7. How did WMCA in New York affect the release date of the soundtrack album to the Beatles' first movie, *A Hard Day's Night*?

8. The Who's 1967 *Sell Out* album was set up as a sly tribute to what British radio broadcasters?

9. What was the Cruisin' record album series, first issued in 1970?

10. What did the weekly *American Top 40* show use to determine the top-selling singles in the United States?

11. What syndicated series (beginning in the 1970s) show-cased the "demented" tastes of record collector Barry Hansen, who enthusiastically touted such offbeat record-ings as "Shaving Cream" and "They're Coming To Take Me Away, Ha-Haa!"?

12. Identify the artists on each of these radio-related hit rec-ords of the 1970s:
"You Turn Me On, I'm a Radio" (1973)
"W.O.L.D." (1974)
"FM (No Static at All)" (1978)
"Life Is a Rock (But the Radio Rolled Me)" (1974)

13. In 1981, Dick Clark produced and hosted a three-hour musical history of the Beach Boys that aired over the Me-morial Day weekend on Mutual. What weekly series de-veloped out of this?

14. In a three-hour radio special aired on Memorial Day weekend in 1982, Beatles fans were treated to dozens of previously unreleased recordings by the group. What was the source of the material?

15. In the summer of 1983, the ABC FM network began a series of weekly one-hour programs tracing the history of the Beatles. What former member of the group served as host?

16. What was the oddly appropriate inaugural song played on MTV (Music Television), the cable music service launched in 1981 as a video equivalent to rock radio?

ANSWERS

1. *Rick Nelson, who played himself on* The Adventures of Ozzie and Harriet *beginning in 1949. He actually launched his singing career on the television version of the show, quickly becoming one of rock's most consistent hit-makers. He landed more than a dozen records in the top ten during his heyday in the late 1950s and early 1960s, including "Poor Little Fool" in 1958, "For You" in 1964, and (a comeback hit) "Garden Party" in 1972.*

2. *"The Flying Saucers" (also called "Back to Earth"). The track was set up as a rock radio broadcast with a disc jockey who handed over the mike to "John Cameron Cameron" for an on-the-spot report concerning a flying saucer landing on Earth. Throughout the piece, Buchanan and Goodman would break in with excerpts from other records, using them both as tunes played by the DJ and as lines of dialogue in the story. As a result, this type of release became known as a break-in record. They released several more over the next two decades, usually making use of contemporary parody hooks such as TV's* Untouchables *and* Batman, Superfly, *and the Watergate hearings.*

3. *WINS. The station became the first in New York to succeed with a rock 'n' roll format. Freed, also known as the Moondog, had been playing early rock for a few years on WJW in Cleveland. On September 6, 1954, Freed began doing a similar show on WINS from 4:00 to 5:00 P.M. and from 11:00 P.M. to 2:00 A.M. Freed's New York shows were also syndicated to sixty other stations. He came to network radio in March 1956 with* Rock 'n' Roll Dance Party, *a thirty-minute Saturday night music show for CBS, on which his co-host was Count Basie.*

4. *Freed had been indicted for inciting a riot in Boston during one of his traveling rock 'n' roll shows on May 3, 1958, so WINS "temporarily" suspended him. In response, Freed quit the station and* joined rival rocker *WABC* on June 2, taking the 7:15-to-11:00 weeknight slot. He also signed with *WABD-TV* (soon renamed *WNEW-TV*) for a 5:00-to-6:00 weekday local *TV* version of American Bandstand *called* Alan Freed's Big Beat Party, *beginning on June 30.*

5. *The "payola" scandal. Freed refused to sign a statement that he had never received payola (inducements from record companies to play their records), so he was fired by WABC on November 20, 1959. He was also fired by WNEW-TV, which aired his last video program on November 28, 1959.*

6. *George Carlin. One routine was included on his* Take-Offs and Put-Ons *album during the late 1960s. He revisited the station on the "Son of WINO" track from his 1972 album* FM & AM.

7. *The release date was moved up when WMCA got hold of the album and played it in its entirety on June 25, 1964—ten days before the scheduled release. To meet the demands of the public and other radio stations, United Artists advanced its schedule and shipped copies to stores on June 26.*

8. *So-called pirate radio stations. At the time, there were only a limited number of outlets for rock music on the BBC in Britain, so independent programmers set up offshore transmission points, which were affectionately dubbed pirates.* The Who Sell Out *was a tribute to their enterprise. Along with such songs as the hit "I Can See For Miles," the album included station jingles, commercials, and public service announcements staged especially for the disc. After a few years, pressure from official channels shut down the pirates, though the BBC substantially increased its own rock music programming in the process.*

9. *The Cruisin' albums presented the history of U.S. rock radio on a series of seven discs, each focusing on one year (from 1956 to 1962). Each volume featured an appropriate disc jockey of the era recreating one of his shows: playing records, doing commercials, and even plugging his latest sock hop appearance. Additional volumes in the series were released in 1972 (covering 1955 and 1963) and 1973 (covering 1964 to 1967). The disc jockeys featured on each disc were:*
1955: "Jumpin' " George Oxford (KSAN, San Francisco)

1956: Robin Seymour (WKMH, Detroit)
1957: Joe Niagara (WIBG, Philadelphia)
1958: Jack Carney (WIL, St. Louis)
1959: Hunter Hancock (KGFJ, Los Angeles)
1960: Dick Biondi (WKBW, Buffalo)
1961: Arnie "Woo Woo" Ginsburg (WMEX, Boston)
1962: Russ "Weird Beard" Knight (KLIF, Dallas)
1963: B. Mitchell Reed (WMCA, New York)
1964: Johnny Holliday (WHK, Cleveland)
1965: Robert W. Morgan (KHJ, Los Angeles)
1966: Pat O'Day (KJR, Seattle)
1967: Dr. Don Rose (WQXI, Atlanta)
The project was conceived by Ron Jacobs.

10. *The "Hot 100" chart published in* Billboard *magazine. Actually,* Billboard *was even more important to American Top 40 as a key to the past. Because the magazine (and its sales charts) had been around long before the first rock hits of the 1950s, its charts provided a wealth of historical statistics to compare with current favorites. That way, records on the way up were out to beat not only contemporary leaders, but also some of pop music's biggest hits of the past.*

11. Dr. Demento. *Hansen used Dr. Demento as his on-air moniker.*

12. *Joni Mitchell did "You Turn Me On, I'm a Radio"*
Harry Chapin did "W.O.L.D."
Steely Dan did "FM (No Static at All)"
Reunion did "Life Is a Rock (But the Radio Rolled Me)."
The first three songs were straightforward pop tunes that happened to be about radio. The last song, however, was an odd novelty hit. The record consisted of a chant (to a backbeat) listing rock personalities, song titles, and odd memory hooks from the rock era. There were even some customized mixes of the single for major stations throughout the country, in which the title was changed to include individual call letters, such as "Life Is a Rock (But WLS Rolled Me)" for WLS in Chicago.

13. Dick Clark's National Music Survey. *The three-hour program played the top album and single hits in the nation along with narration and interviews by Dick Clark.*

14. *The BBC in England.* From 1962 to 1965, the Beatles appeared on more than fifty radio shows for the BBC. At the time, there was a tremendous emphasis at the BBC on musicians performing live from the radio studio rather than disc jockeys merely spinning the latest record release. As a result, the Beatles not only gave fresh performances of their own commercial hits such as "Please Please Me" and "She Loves You," but also presented material that they never released on discs—usually their interpretations of songs written by other artists (such as Chuck Berry's "Sweet Little Sixteen" or Buddy Holly's "Crying, Waiting, Hoping"). Recordings of this material stayed on the BBC's shelves for nearly two decades, but were dusted off in the early 1980s in response to growing nostalgic interest in the group. Instead of just releasing the songs on discs, though, the BBC chose to put together a full-fledged radio special incorporating the music along with background narration. The special played in England on March 7, 1982, to celebrate the twentieth anniversary of the group's first BBC radio appearance. Later in the year, the package was syndicated to individual stations throughout the United States, airing on most during the Memorial Day weekend.

15. *Ringo Starr.* The series was dubbed Ringo's Yellow Submarine: A Voyage Through Beatles Magic.

16. *"Video Killed the Radio Star" by the Buggles.* The song bemoaned the destructive effects of television and video tape recorders on radio. A few years earlier, the record had been a big hit in England and the rest of Europe, but it had never really caught on in the United States. Ironically, then, the song reached its biggest Stateside audience through the MTV video presentation.

Radio TV

1. Though Bob Hope was one of the first comics to jump into television in the early 1950s, he also continued to perform on radio. Beginning in 1952, he even added a five-times-a-week daytime series for NBC. What did this new radio show consist of?

2. When *Amos and Andy* moved to television in 1950, who were the only two radio performers to make the crossover to TV?

3. When *The George Burns and Gracie Allen Show* came to television in 1950, who played neighbors Blanche and Harry Morton?

4. When *Our Miss Brooks* went to television in 1952, all but one of the radio leads made the transition to TV. What major character was recast?

5. When *Father Knows Best* came to television in 1954 after five years on radio, who was the only radio cast member to make the switch?

6. What CBS television drama anthology began on radio in 1947, the year before its video premiere?

7. In a reversal of the more common trend of the 1950s, the television hits *My Little Margie* and *Have Gun, Will Travel* set up radio versions. Which one did not bring along its TV leads?

8. What was the first show to return to radio after the success of a television version?

9. What television space adventure added a radio version in 1952, with the TV cast continuing in the leading roles?

10. What cowboy hero won his own radio show in the early 1950s following the successful repackaging of his films from the 1930s and 1940s for early television?

11. Shortly before starring in television's *I Love Lucy,* Desi Arnaz had his own CBS radio music series. Name the show.

12. Name the TV comedy star of the 1950s who began his network radio career in the mid-1940s as co-host to a comedy-variety show with Les Tremayne.

13. Name the young comic who served as Jack Benny's summer replacement in 1947 and later became one of the top TV variety hosts of the late 1950s and early 1960s.

14. On November 25, 1960, *Amos and Andy* ended more than thirty years on radio. The following fall, however, very similar characters came to prime-time television in an animated cartoon format. What was the show?

15. In 1966, Bud Collyer, the voice of Superman for the 1940s radio series, returned to the mike once again as the man of steel. What was the occasion?

16. Name the 1967 CBS television sit-com about a disc jockey team (Lewis and Clarke) working the morning shift at a Los Angeles radio station.

17. Name the CBS television series that ran for four seasons (beginning in 1978) and followed the rise of a low-rated midwestern radio station to the top ten in its market.

18. Name the 1979 NBC television series starring McLean Stevenson as Larry Adler, a radio call-in host who moved his program and family from Los Angeles to Portland, Oregon, following his divorce.

19. What late night television comedy-variety series instituted a radio simulcast in the fall of 1981?

20. What radio network began offering an audio version of *Monday Night Football* in 1972?

ANSWERS

1. *A straightforward monologue that ran about fifteen minutes. There were no complicated skits or big-budget guest star numbers, just a well-oiled solo performance by Hope, aimed at the housewife audience.*

2. *Ernestine Wade who played Sapphire Stevens, wife of the Kingfish, and Amanda Randolph, who played Sapphire's mother.*

3. *Bea Benaderet and Hal March, the same performers who played the roles on radio. Another radio holdover was announcer Bill Goodwin. However, March and Goodwin soon left the video version and were replaced by Harry Von Zell and Fred Clark (later Larry Keating). This supporting cast was in place when the* Burns and Allen *TV series went from live performances to film, and so became the most familiar figures to subsequent viewers through continued reruns of the series in syndication since the 1950s.*

4. *Philip Boynton. Jeff Chandler played him on radio. Robert Rockwell took the role for the television version. The character never popped the question in either run, though he did at last propose marriage to Miss Brooks in a theatrical film version of the series.*

5. *Robert Young as Jim Anderson, the wise and patient father.*

6. Studio One. *The series premiered on CBS radio with an exciting adaptation of Malcolm Lowrey's* Under the Volcano *on April 29, 1947. Studio One never really gained much of a foothold on radio but built its fame as a television series beginning in 1948.*

7. Have Gun, Will Travel, *which cast John Dehner in Richard Boone's role as Paladin. That series ran on radio until the fall of 1960, while* My Little Margie *was gone by 1955.*

8. The Original Amateur Hour. *The series had played on NBC*

from 1935 to 1936, then on CBS from 1936 to 1945, when its longtime host Major Edward Bowes died. In January 1948, Bowes's protégé Ted Mack revived the show on DuMont television, and its popularity brought the program back to network radio on September 18, 1948, for ABC. This radio version lasted until 1952.

 9. Tom Corbett, Space Cadet, *with Frankie Thomas as Tom, Al Markim as Astro, Jan Merlin as Roger, and Ed Bryce as their mentor, Captain Strong.*

10. *Hopalong Cassidy.*

11. Your Tropical Trip. *This weekly half-hour of infectious Latin rhythms ran on Sunday afternoons from January to April 1951.*

12. *Jackie Gleason. On August 13, 1944, the* Jackie Gleason–Les Tremayne Show *premiered on NBC radio at 10:30* P.M. *on Sundays. Gleason had earned the slot after starring in a Broadway hit,* Follow the Girls *and a local New York radio program,* The Keep Ahead Show, *on WOR.*

13. *Jack Paar. He took over Benny's choice Sunday slot at 7:00* P.M. *on NBC in June 1947, after attracting attention as a guest on Vaughn Monroe's program. Paar did well in his summer stint, and in November landed a prime time slot on ABC.*

14. Calvin and the Colonel, *which played for one season on ABC beginning in the fall of 1961. Freeman Gosden did the voice for Colonel Montgomery J. Klaxton, and Charles Correll did the same for Calvin Burnside. The program neatly avoided any charges of racial stereotyping, which had become an issue with the television version of* Amos and Andy, *by making the cartoon characters noncontroversial humanized animals. Calvin was a bear and the Colonel was a fox.*

15. *A CBS Saturday morning television cartoon series called* The New Adventures of Superman. *Collyer even recorded the vocals for the new program in one of the old studios used for the radio series. Appropriately, the TV cartoon series was a smash hit, introducing radio's Superman to the Saturday morning cartoon crowd.*

16. Good Morning World. *Joby Baker and Ronnie Schell played Dave Lewis and Larry Clarke. Goldie Hawn was in the supporting*

cast as a gossipy next-door neighbor with her eye on bachelor Larry. The series lasted only one season.

17. WKRP in Cincinnati.

18. Hello, Larry. *Larry Adler's talk show played on the mythical Portland station KLOW.* Hello, Larry *was produced by the same company that did the popular* Diff'rent Strokes *TV series, so the characters sometimes appeared on each other's shows. That was not enough for* Hello, Larry, *though, and the show was gone by the spring of 1980.*

19. *NBC's* Saturday Night Live. *This was part of an overall rebuilding effort after one disastrous season following the departure of the original cast and producer. Emphasizing guests from the world of rock on the program, an ad hoc network of stations began carrying an audio simulcast of the show in the fall of 1981. This was wisely dropped almost immediately, however, as much of the show made absolutely no sense without the visuals.*

20. *Mutual. Two years after ABC began its series of Monday night television broadcasts of NFL contests, Mutual began radio coverage of the games, featuring Van Patrick and Al Wester. Football fans who did not like ABC's Howard Cosell on the television coverage could turn their TV volume down and listen to the audio from the radio instead. In 1978, CBS outbid Mutual for radio rights to the Monday games.*

Vinyl Review

1. In the fall of 1950, NBC launched a flashy ninety-minute series aimed at competing directly with television for the big-budget variety audience. Name this program.

2. Name the two famous disc jockey pairs who came to national radio in the summer of 1951, after moving from successful local shows (one in Boston, the other in New York).

3. Name satirist Stan Freberg's first network radio series.

4. After more than twenty-five years with NBC, why did *The Voice of Firestone* jump to ABC in 1954?

5. What top-rated TV quiz show of the mid-1950s flopped as a radio simulcast?

6. Name the NBC radio show that TV quiz star Charles Van Doren appeared on in 1957.

7. What was the most expensive giveaway quiz show ever produced by a radio network?

8. In April 1953, disc jockey Alan Freed was involved in a serious accident. What happened?

9. Who was Carol Burnett's co-star in her early 1960s CBS variety series?

10. During the 1950s, NBC presented an adult science fiction anthology series that featured work by such writers as Ray Bradbury, Isaac Asimov, and Robert Bloch. What was it called?

11. In December 1955, NBC's *Dragnet* came in fourteenth for the week in the overall radio ratings. What shift did this signal for prime time radio?

12. What radio veteran produced and directed NBC's 1959 daily drama anthology series, *The NBC Radio Theater*?

13. Name the weekday radio drama anthology program that ran on ABC during 1964 and 1965.

14. In the late 1960s, the West Coast–based Firesign Theatre comedy troupe put on record a full-fledged radio crime drama parody. Name the title character.

15. Who was the wonderful white-winged weekend warrior first introduced to radio audiences in 1966 as "the most fantastic crime fighter the world has ever known"?

16. Name both the CBS and the NBC series of five-minute feature reports that played throughout the day during the 1960s.

17. What famous newspaper advice columnist had a similar radio feature on CBS in the 1960s and 1970s?

18. What former New York Yankee shortstop had a long-running nightly sports show on CBS from the 1950s to the 1970s?

19. Give the title and host of CBS's fifteen-minute evening sports wrapup of the 1960s.

20. What were the first two commercial FM stations to test stereo broadcasting?

21. How did a 1967 FCC rule foster the growth of "progressive" FM radio programming?

22. Name the 1968 novelty record by Guy Marks that was presented as a nostalgic "live" big band radio broadcast from the Hotel Sheets in downtown Plunketville.

23. What made November 28, 1960, a watershed date for CBS radio?

24. What was special about the economic picture for CBS, NBC, ABC, and Mutual radio in 1965?

ANSWERS

1. The Big Show. *The series aired on Sundays from 6:00 to 7:30 P.M. with Tallulah Bankhead as host.* The Big Show *not only attempted to match the glitter of TV variety (which had lured a host of big-name radio stars to headline programs in the fall of 1950), but also represented NBC's first serious effort to challenge Jack Benny's domination of that time period on radio. Though the program received great reviews and even traveled to London and Paris during its second season, it could not attract sufficient sponsor support to carry its huge budget. The big commercial money had gone to TV. NBC lost about $1 million on the series over its two-year run, which ended on April 20, 1952.*

2. *Bob Goulding and Ray Elliot, and Gene Rayburn and Dee Finch.* The Bob and Ray Show *premiered on NBC on July 2 as a fifteen-minute weekday afternoon series, while* The Rayburn and Finch Show *premiered on CBS on June 22 on Friday nights. Bob and Ray had been successful on WHDH in Boston, while Rayburn and Finch had been local New York celebrities and had briefly appeared on an ABC network series in the summer of 1950. As more and more big-name artists left radio for television, the radio networks turned to such personable disc jockeys to fill the air with recorded music and light banter.*

3. That's Rich. *The program was a short-lived half-hour sit-com that premiered on CBS in January 1954 and featured Freberg as a bird watcher. By then, he had already earned a reputation as a media satirist with his takeoffs (on record) of radio soap operas (John and Marsha in 1950) and Dragnet (St. George and the Dragonet in 1953). Still, his best radio work came three years later on* The Stan Freberg Show, *a Sunday night series that ran for one summer on CBS. Freberg released an album containing highlights of that 1957 program soon after the show was axed.*

4. *NBC wanted to move the show from its longtime Monday night position because of the weak ratings of the television simulcast version. Fighting this, the program jumped to ABC and retained its slot on Monday night at 8:30.*

5. The $64,000 Question on *CBS. The program premiered on television in June 1955 and quickly became the top-rated show on television. A CBS radio simulcast of the live TV proceedings began on October 4, 1955, but lasted only two months. Apparently the folks at home needed to see the quiz contestants in the isolation booth.*

6. Conversation, *a thirty-minute Thursday night discussion program. During Charles Van Doren's appearance in March 1957, he and host Clifton Fadiman chewed over the question, "What is an educated man?" Two and one-half years later, Van Doren offered far more startling insights when he admitted in congressional testimony that his quiz show successes had been rigged.*

7. Million Dollar Quiz, *produced by Mutual. However, it never aired. Mutual had been in the forefront of the giveaway quiz show trend of the late 1940s with such programs as* Break the Bank, *and, when such series caught on again in the mid-1950s on television, the network planned a new radio quiz, with a top prize of one million dollars. However, Mutual never brought the show beyond the pilot stage, airing only a three-week trial run in March 1957 under the title* Sounds in Action *(hosted by Bob and Ray). Even this appeared on only one station, WJOC in Jamestown, New York. No one ever received a million dollar prize.*

8. *He was seriously injured in a car crash. In 1953, Freed was working for Cleveland station WJW doing a Monday-through-Saturday music show. After one late night shift, he fell asleep at the wheel of his car and crashed. Though seriously injured, he recovered relatively quickly and, the following year, headed for New York, where he became one of the key disc jockeys in the country who popularized the black-based rock 'n' roll sound that was just then beginning to emerge from rhythm and blues music.*

9. *Richard Hayes. The* Carol Burnett–Richard Hayes Show *ran for twenty minutes each weekday evening on CBS, beginning on September 4, 1961.*

10. Dimension X, *which played in the early 1950s. NBC revived the* *show as* X Minus One, *from 1955 to 1958 and then again from 1973 to 1975.*

11. *The fact that daytime programming had replaced nighttime programming as radio's prime time.* Dragnet *was the highest rated nighttime radio series of the week, meaning that, for the first time in radio history, there were no evening series in the top ten. This shift was due to the advent of television, which had come to dominate evening entertainment by the mid-1950s.*

12. *Himan Brown. The program failed to take hold in the dying days of radio drama, but Brown returned again in the 1970s with* The CBS Radio Mystery Theater.

13. Theater Five. *The series presented new twenty-five-minute dramas on ABC until June 1965.*

14. *Nick Danger. The twenty-eight-minute "Further Adventures of Nick Danger" appeared on the Firesign Theatre's 1969 album* How Can You Be in Two Places at Once When You're Not Anywhere at All? *and proved to be their most popular skit ever. Ten years later they at last recorded a follow-up adventure, "The Case of the Missing Shoe," for distribution first as a five-episode radio mini-series, then on an album called simply* Nick Danger.

15. *Chickenman alias Benton Harbor—both identities alias Dick Orkin, who created the character and did the main voices. The adventures of Chickenman caught on in the aftermath of the spectacular success on television of ABC's* Batman. Chickenman *played five days a week in short humorous vignettes that were syndicated from Chicago for about a year. The program was revived for a few years in the 1970s in another syndicated package. Chickenman was known as the weekend warrior because he had time to fight crime and/or evil only on Saturday and Sunday. The rest of the week, Benton Harbor worked as a department store shoe salesman.*

16. *CBS had* Dimension, *which began in 1962. NBC had* Emphasis, *which began in 1963.*

17. *Abigail Van Buren. She hosted* Dear Abby *on CBS for eleven years, from December 31, 1963 to December 27, 1974.*

18. *Phil Rizzuto. His series,* It's Sports Time, *ran on CBS from 1957 to 1976.*

19. World Wide Sports. *The program began on May 28, 1962, with Chris Schenkel as host. When Schenkel defected to ABC at the end of 1964, Frank Gifford replaced him.*

20. *WCRB-FM and WBZ-FM in Boston. Both began a series of test stereo broadcasts in May 1960.*

21. *As of January 1, 1967, the FCC required each FM station owned by an AM station (in cities with more than 100,000 people) to do at least 50 percent original programming. Until then, most such "sister" FM stations had merely carried a simulcast of the AM signal. By requiring independent programming for FM, the FCC forced the station owners to turn to other types of programming. This helped foster the growth of the eclectic "underground" FM rock music stations of the late 1960s, which offered relatively cheap programming with their long stretches of time filled with obscure album tracks. One of the first such stations on the East Coast was WOR-FM in New York, which ran a progressive rock format from mid-1966 to November 1967. Another New York station, WNEW-FM, adopted that format as well in October 1967, but to much greater commercial success.*

22. Loving You Has Made Me Bananas. *The announcer at the opening of the track described the musical "interlude" as a medley of old standards: "Your Red Scarf Matches Your Eyes," "Close Cover before Striking," "Your Father Had the Shipfitter Blues," and "Loving You Has Made Me Bananas."*

23. *It marked the start of CBS's new radio schedule, which eliminated all soap operas and most entertainment shows, emphasizing instead news and features. This was the long-postponed admission that the approach taken to network radio during the 1930s and 1940s no longer applied in the 1960s. On November 25, 1960, CBS aired the last episodes of eight afternoon and evening series that had run for years under its previous schedule:*
    12:30–12:45 The Couple Next Door *(on since 1958)*
    12:45–1:00 The Right to Happiness *(on since 1939)*
    1:05–1:15 Whispering Streets *(on since 1952)*
    1:15–1:30 Ma Perkins *(on since 1933)*
    1:30–1:45 Young Dr. Malone *(on since 1939)*
    1:45–2:00 The Second Mrs. Burton *(on since 1946)*

7:05-7:25 Amos and Andy *(on since 1929)*
The last Have Gun, Will Travel *(on since 1958) aired on Sunday, November 27. On Monday, November 28, 1960, CBS expanded its news on the hour from five to ten minutes and put in a series of five-minute news features at half-past the hour.*

Over the next two years, CBS completed its purge, dropping Gunsmoke *on June 18, 1961, and its last two dramatic series,* Suspense *and* Yours Truly, Johnny Dollar, *in October 1962. That left only* House Party, *which ran until October 13, 1967, and Arthur Godfrey, who stayed on until his retirement on April 30, 1972.*

24. *For the first time since 1954, all four radio networks made money. Since the rise of television in the early 1950s, radio profits had taken a nose dive. As they moved into the '60s, the networks had been forced to revamp their basic approach to programming. Once the changes were in place, though, they began turning a profit once again.*

AND NOW
THE NEWS

And Now the News

1. What aircraft disaster was vividly described by a radio announcer as it happened on May 6, 1937?

2. What popular columnist began his radio broadcasts with the greeting: "Good evening, Mr. and Mrs. North and South America and all ships at sea. Let's go to press—Flash!"?

3. During CBS's coverage of the funeral of President Franklin D. Roosevelt, what announcer shared his personal emotions with millions of listeners, actually breaking down and crying on the air?

4. When listeners tuned in to *Wendy Warren and the News* beginning in 1947 on CBS, what did they hear in addition to the latest headline reports?

5. From its beginning in 1931, how did *The March of Time* manage to present the sounds and voices from worldwide news events virtually as they happened?

6. What famous Edward R. Murrow series began as a phonograph record?

7. What famous news commentator was the first to broadcast on-the-spot news coverage of a battle over American radio?

8. Who was Eleanor Roosevelt's co-host for her commentary series of the late 1940s?

9. What news event resulted in the birth of CBS's long-running *World News Roundup* program?

10. Name CBS's nighttime equivalent to its morning news show, the *CBS World News Roundup.*

11. Name Mutual's evening news roundup show that began in 1958.

12. What brought Chicago-based commentator Paul Harvey to national attention shortly after he began his long-running program on ABC?

13. What CBS drama series recreated important moments in world history by covering them as developing news events, complete with appropriate "on-the-spot" sounds and interviews with participants?

14. Who produced and sponsored the weekly *March of Time* series?

15. What was the name of NBC's weekend-long news, information, and entertainment package that began in the mid-1950s?

16. What was NBC's *Weekday* series from the mid-1950s?

17. Who was the host of *Flair*, ABC's early 1960s equivalent of NBC's *Monitor*?

18. What did the title of NBC's documentary series, *Second Sunday*, refer to?

19. What was peculiar about the scheduling of *Perspective*, ABC's commentary and feature program that began in 1967?

20. Name Mike Wallace's interview program that began on CBS in the mid-1960s.

21. What was the first network to present a five-minute news update every hour.

22. What was the first network to offer on-the-hour news twenty-four hours a day?

23. What was the first network series devoted exclusively to coverage of the war in Vietnam?

24. What was NBC's "News and Information Service"?

25. Name National Public Radio's ninety-minute evening news and features program.

26. Name National Public Radio's morning news and features program.

27. What was the first American radio station to adopt an "all-news" format?

28. What did Ted Turner use as the basis for an all-news radio network in 1982?

29. Why did the CBS-owned and -operated radio stations do away with their *Music till Dawn* late night series in January 1970?

30. What program replaced *Walter Cronkite Reporting* on CBS in early 1981?

ANSWERS

1. *The crash of the German zeppelin* Hindenburg *as it attempted to land at Lakehurst, New Jersey. Reporter Herb Morrison was there to record a test program for a proposed series when the zeppelin suddenly burst into flame right before his eyes. Horrified, he nonetheless described the terrifying situation, pausing several times to regain his composure. The recording of Morrison's description of the crash was quickly put on the air and played to a shocked radio audience. Thirty-six people died in the accident.*

2. *Walter Winchell. He also had rapid-fire telegraph tappings as accompaniment to his commentaries.*

3. *Arthur Godfrey. His sincere and open reactions to a very emotional situation made him an instant friend to millions who shared his feelings.*

4. *A soap opera. The program was cleverly designed to lure people who would normally never consider following a soap by beginning each broadcast with a real newscast, read by Douglas Edwards. Then Wendy (played by Florence Freeman) would do stories "for women" (fashion news and such). After about five minutes of this, Wendy would step from the announcing booth into that day's soapy adventures.*

5. *The news stories were actually dramatizations based on reports and information filed by the program's correspondents. Actors impersonated political figures such as Franklin Roosevelt and Adolf Hitler, while the sound effects engineers recreated everything from a war front to a baseball game. By the 1940s, advances in technology allowed the program to place far greater emphasis on news actualities (sound recorded on the scene) rather than on dramatizations.*

6. Hear It Now. *In November 1948, Murrow and NBC producer*

Fred W. Friendly released a documentary record I Can Hear It Now, *which collected the sounds of major news events from 1933 to 1945. The success of that record, and of a second volume released in November 1949 (covering 1945 to 1949), brought Friendly over to CBS, where he joined Murrow for a weekly* Hear It Now *magazine-style program beginning in December 1950. The program was far more successful on CBS television as* See It Now, *which ran from 1951 to 1958.*

7. *H. V. Kaltenborn. He sent in some dramatic on-the-spot reports of the battle of Irun in 1936 during the Spanish Civil War. Previously, such foreign stories had been transmitted Stateside and then read by announcers in the studio.*

8. *Anna Roosevelt Boettiger, her daughter. Eleanor Roosevelt handled the strong political commentary while Anna focused on softer feature items.*

9. *The Nazi takeover of Austria on March 13, 1938. To cover the fast-breaking story, CBS put together reports from its available personnel in European capitals. One correspondent was Edward R. Murrow, who made his broadcast debut with the program. The* CBS World News Roundup *continued after the Austrian crisis and was the main force in popularizing on-the-spot reporting over just a studio announcer reading text items transmitted from the overseas correspondents. By the 1950s, the* CBS World News Roundup *had become CBS's primary morning news program and was anchored, from the late 1950s to the early 1980s, by Dallas Townsend.*

10. The World Tonight. *The series premiered in the fall of 1956 as a twenty-minute review of the day's news. It was later reduced to fifteen minutes each night.*

11. The World Today. *The series premiered in June 1958 as a twenty-five-minute nightly news program anchored by Westbrook Van Voorhis, formerly of the* March of Time.

12. *Paul Harvey was arrested on February 6, 1951, for sneaking into the Argonne Atomic Lab in Lemont, Illinois, to demonstrate the lab's lax security. He was brought before a grand jury, but no indictments resulted. Harvey's national radio program began a few months before that (December 3, 1950) and ran on Sunday nights on ABC.*

13. You Are There. *The series was created by Goodman Ace and played on CBS from 1946 to 1950. Network news reporters such as John Daly participated in the broadcasts. When the series came to television in the 1950s, Walter Cronkite served as its chief historical correspondent.*

14. Time *magazine. Though there were a few other sponsors for a brief time in the mid-1930s, Time maintained production and editorial control throughout the entire run of the series, from 1931 to 1945.*

15. Monitor. *The program was, in several ways, a radio equivalent to NBC-TV's Today show, in that it combined news, interviews, features, music, and disc jockey chat. Like Today, Monitor was brought to the air through the efforts of NBC president Sylvester "Pat" Weaver, premiering on June 12, 1955. The show represented a radical break from previous scheduling practices for network radio by replacing separate shows featuring individual hosts with a national weekend radio service that ran from 8:00 A.M. Saturday through midnight Sunday. The program flourished through the 1960s, then faded in the 1970s as all-news radio stations took much of its thunder. Many affiliates dropped all but a few hours of the show. NBC ended the series in February 1975, but revived the Monitor title in 1983 for a weekly television news magazine.*

16. *An attempt to place the lengthy, flexible Monitor format into the weekday schedule. The program began on November 7, 1955, with a five-hour package spread out between 10:00 A.M. and 6:00 P.M. That was cut to two hours in July 1956 and then in September* Weekday *was dropped completely. Mike Wallace and Margaret Truman acted as hosts.*

17. Dick Van Dyke. *Flair premiered on October 3, 1960, as a fifty-five-minute weekday afternoon disc jockey and feature show for ABC. The program lasted until July 1963, by which time Van Dyke had become the star of his own television sit-com. The Flair title lived on for a few more years as Flair Reports, a series of five-minute features that aired throughout ABC's weekday schedule.*

18. *The day on which the program aired. The fifty-five-minute Second Sunday ran on the second Sunday of the month, from October 1966 to December 1982.*

19. *The show was presented in two twenty-five-minute segments, interrupted by a five-minute newscast. Some stations wanting less than an hour of public affairs from the block aired only one part of the show, certainly confusing listeners who heard references to previous or upcoming reports.*

20. Mike Wallace at Large. *The program premiered as a twenty-five-minute once-a-week program in the fall of 1965. By the 1970s, the show was split into five five-minute reports that aired each weekday. In January 1979 the series moved to weekends where it aired twice each day.*

21. *ABC. In 1954, the network filled weekends with the hourly news reports to better fit in with the increasingly independent nature of the local affiliates. By the late 1950s, all the radio networks had adopted the on-the-hour news update.*

22. *CBS. The twenty-four-hour service began on April 2, 1973. Prior to that, CBS's on-the-hour news ran from 6:00 A.M. to 1:00 A.M. Monday through Friday; 7:00 A.M. to 1:00 A.M. on Saturday; and 8:00 A.M. to 1:00 A.M. on Sunday. NBC went to a twenty-four-hour service on January 1, 1974.*

23. Vietnam Update. *This weekly report on the war premiered on ABC on November 19, 1965.*

24. *An all-news radio network. The service premiered on June 18, 1975, over thirty-three stations and died on May 29, 1977. NBC explained that it needed 150 stations to carry it in order to make money on the project, but only sixty-two stations were signed on when the decision was made to end it.*

25. All Things Considered. *The program premiered on May 3, 1971, over 112 stations.*

26. Morning Edition. *The program premiered in 1979 as a morning equivalent to the network's popular* All Things Considered.

27. *WMIN in Minneapolis–St. Paul. The station did eighteen hours of news each day from July to September 1962. Before that, however, XTRA in Tijuana, Mexico, set up an all-news format that reached the Los Angeles area. In the States, a small station in Chicago tried an all-news format in September 1964, dubbing itself WNUS. The first major station to go all news was a New York City* rock station, *Westinghouse's WINS, which converted to news on April 19, 1965. Another Westinghouse station, KYW in Philadelphia, followed in September 1965. The first network-owned station to try the all-news format was WCBS in New York, beginning on August 18, 1967.*

28. *He offered radio stations the audio portion of his television CNN Headline Service.*

29. *In the late 1960s, virtually all CBS-owned and -operated AM stations adopted a news and talk format. This even extended into the overnight hours, so* Music till Dawn *had to go. Thus, the sixteen-year policy of playing "soothing" music all night long gave way to news capsules, weather updates, and sports roundups.*

30. Dan Rather Reporting. *At the time, Dan Rather also replaced Walter Cronkite as anchor of CBS's nightly television news show.*

THE SATELLITE AGE

Radio Film
Radio Talk
Satellite Review

Radio Film

1. What real-life disc jockey played himself in the 1973 film *American Graffiti*?

2. Both the 1957 *Mr. Rock and Roll* and the 1978 *American Hot Wax* theatrical feature films focused on the activities of what 1950s radio personality?

3. What 1978 feature film presented the struggles of an independent radio station attempting to fight off the pressures of the commercial world?

4. What 1977 feature film starring Paul LeMat and Candy Clark used CB radio to tie together its loose plot lines and character vignettes?

5. Name the 1970 feature film about a superpatriotic radio station, starring Paul Newman and Joanne Woodward.

6. Name the 1950 theatrical film with Nancy Davis (Reagan) and James Whitmore that presented the most dynamic of all radio personalities—God.

7. Name the 1940 comedy-thriller film in which Bob Hope played a radio "crime gossip" host, Lawrence Lawrence, who investigated a haunted mansion in Cuba.

8. Name the 1930 theatrical film featuring Amos and Andy, played by Freeman Gosden and Charles Correll (in blackface).

ANSWERS

1. *Wolfman Jack.*

2. *Alan Freed. The 1957 film featured Freed playing himself, while the 1978 offering had Tim McIntire in that role.*

3. FM.

4. Citizens Band. *After an unsuccessful initial release, the title was changed to* Handle with Care *in an attempt to distinguish it from other quickie merchandising cash-ins on the CB radio craze.*

5. WUSA.

6. The Next Voice You Hear. *In the film, God decided that it was time to speak directly to the people, so he arranged for his voice to come over the radio.*

7. Ghost Breakers. *Hope's character touted himself as "the man who knows all the rackets and all the racketeers" and who was not afraid to broadcast his gossipy scoops on the air. Naturally, this led to trouble with the underworld, a lady in distress, and some cute digs at radio programs and commercials along the way. This was one of Hope's best films of the era; he has strong support from Richard Carlson, Paul Lukas, Willie Best, Anthony Quinn, and co-star Paulette Goddard (as the heiress to the haunted mansion).*

8. Check and Double Check.

Radio Talk

1. What was the first all-night network call-in program?

2. In what city did *The Larry King Show* originate?

3. What was ABC's early 1980s Talkradio service?

4. What was NBC's 1980s attempt at a late night talk show?

5. What was the early 1980s Talknet service?

6. Name RKO's early 1980s late night call-in show.

7. What veteran disc jockey was the host of the early 1980s series *Rockline*, a live national call-in show aimed at young people?

8. How did President Jimmy Carter attempt to communicate directly with the public shortly after his inauguration in 1977?

ANSWERS

1. The Herb Jepko Show. *The program began in 1963 as* Nightcap, *a local offering on KSL in Salt Lake City. As a clear-channel station, KSL's nighttime signal could be heard all over the western two-thirds of the nation, so* Nightcap's *callers came from areas beyond Salt Lake City. In the early 1970s, stations in Baltimore, Louisville, Denver, Seattle, and Los Angeles began carrying the show live, creating an ad hoc national* Nightcap *network. On November 3, 1975, Mutual picked up the show, thus allowing the network to expand to a twenty-four-hour programming schedule. The unusual aspect of Herb Jepko's "national" show was that he rarely had celebrities on and he discouraged callers from talking about politics, preferring instead the more "local" feeling of warm person-to-person chats about what was going on in each caller's life or community.*

2. *Miami. Larry King had been the host of a successful call-in show on WIOD in Miami for a while before he was chosen by Mutual to take over the late night slot previously filled by Herb Jepko (and later by Long John Nebel). King began his 5½ hour post-midnight show for Mutual on January 30, 1978, on just a handful of stations. On April 3, 1978, King moved his show to Mutual's headquarters near Washington, D.C. By 1980, the show was carried on more than two hundred stations.*

3. *ABC's all-talk network. The service began on May 3, 1982, with two ABC West Coast stations, added WABC on May 10, and expanded to a full national network on June 18 with twenty-two stations. Talkradio offered nonstop talk from 10:00 A.M. to 4:00 P.M. and from midnight to 6:00 A.M.*

4. Nightalk. *The program premiered on November 2, 1981. From 10:00 P.M. until midnight, Bruce Williams talked about money mat-*

ters; then Jesse Raphael discussed psychological problems from midnight until 3:00 A.M.

5. *NBC's talk and information service, which began at the end of 1981 and moved to satellite distribution in September 1982.*

6. America Overnight. *The program premiered on September 1, 1981, as a six-hour split between Ed Busch in Dallas (for the first three hours) and Eric Tracy in Los Angeles (for the last three hours). In September 1982, the Los Angeles segment was dropped, and Mitch Carr, also in Dallas, handled the second half of the show. The program disappeared entirely in December 1982, when it was carried by only forty stations.*

7. *B. Mitchell Reed. He conducted the ninety-minute show from ABC's KLOS-FM in Los Angeles, beginning on May 4, 1981, with a network of seventeen stations. Joe Walsh and Tom Johnson were the first guests.*

8. *He took part in a national call-in radio show on CBS,* Ask President Carter. *The program aired live for two hours on a Saturday afternoon in March 1977. Walter Cronkite served as anchor to the show, which was televised on a delayed basis that evening on PBS. Carter participated in another call-in show (for National Public Radio) on October 13, 1978, but for that program callers were selected from questions mailed in advance.*

Satellite Review

1. Who played Luke Skywalker in the National Public Radio–BBC radio production of *Star Wars* and *The Empire Strikes Back*?

2. Who wrote *The Hitch-Hiker's Guide to the Galaxy*?

3. Name the science fiction anthology series NBC revived in 1973.

4. What short-lived spin-off from *CBS Radio Mystery Theater* premiered in early 1977?

5. *Sears Radio Theater,* a weeknight anthology series, began in 1979, presenting a different format with a different host each night. Match the format with the host and the night it aired:

   Adventure   Lorne Greene (Mondays)
   Comedy   Andy Griffith (Tuesdays)
   Love and Hate Drama   Vincent Price (Wednes-
                                days)
   Melodrama   Cicely Tyson (Thursdays)
   Western   Richard Widmark (Fri-
                                days)

6. What radio forum did President Ronald Reagan use to communicate with the American people on a regular basis, beginning on May 3, 1982?

7. When the U.S. House of Representatives at last allowed live radio coverage of its proceedings on June 12, 1978, which major networks carried the opening of that day's sessions?

8. What four separate networks did ABC launch on January 1, 1968?

9. What was "the Source" and how did it originate?

10. What was the name of CBS's youth-oriented radio network of the 1980s?

11. Who was the host of *Movie News* on the ABC-FM network?

12. Who was the host of *Masterpiece Radio Theater*?

13. What network service did National Public Radio replace in 1971?

14. In 1977, the FCC lifted its ban on radio networks offering several different programming services at the same time. What network was the first to take full advantage of the change?

15. Name the two new network program services that ABC put into operation on January 4, 1982.

16. What was the first ethnic-oriented network?

17. When the RKO radio network began programming in 1979, how were most of its shows distributed?

18. What was Mutual's first owned and operated station?

19. What was Superadio?

20. What was the first AM station to broadcast in FCC-approved stereo?

21. What was the name of the short-lived all-sports radio network that began in 1981?

22. Name the host of CBS's weekday radio feature of the early 1980s, *The Subject Is Young People*.

23. Name the co-hosts of *Animal Stories*, a short feature program aired daily on Chicago's WLS beginning in the

24. What claim did NBC make regarding its special *All Star Radio Theater* broadcast of "A Halloween Story" on October 31, 1981?

25. What claim did Mutual make regarding its Sunday afternoon broadcast of the National Symphony on October 17, 1982?

26. On December 18, 1971, CBS ended one of its last connections to radio's "golden age" by discontinuing a once-popular musical programming service. What was it?

27. Why was December 31, 1982, a watershed date for NBC radio?

ANSWERS

1. *Mark Hamill, the same actor who played the role in the film versions.* Star Wars *aired on NPR in early 1981, with* The Empire Strikes Back *following two years later.*

2. *Douglas Adams, who turned out the twelve-part BBC radio series, the seven-episode BBC television version, and the three-volume book adaptation. The radio programs originally aired in Britain in 1978 and 1980, coming to the United States over National Public Radio in 1981. By the end of 1982, all three books had become best-sellers in England and the United States. John Lloyd helped as co-author on episodes five and six of the radio series.*

3. X Minus One. *The program had originally run on NBC from April 1955 to January 1958. In June 1973, NBC began rebroadcasting one episode a month on Sunday evenings. The born-again series was once more put to rest in 1975.*

4. General Mills Adventure Theater. *This fifty-five-minute program was carried by CBS on Saturday and Sunday, beginning February 5, 1977. Himan Brown, producer of* Mystery Theater, *also handled the chores for* Adventure Theater.

5. Sears Radio Theater *formats, hosts, and nights match as follows:*
Western with Lorne Greene (Mondays)
Comedy with Andy Griffith (Tuesdays)
Melodrama with Vincent Price (Wednesdays)
Love and Hate Drama with Cicely Tyson (Thursdays)
Adventure with Richard Widmark (Fridays)
The fifty-five-minute series premiered on February 5, 1979, on CBS, shifted to Mutual on February 1, 1980 (where it became Mutual Radio Theater*), and died on December 19, 1980.*

6. *A series of weekly five-minute Saturday afternoon radio ad-*

dresses to the nation, reminiscent of President Franklin Roosevelt's fireside chats of the 1930s. This time, however, the networks followed President Reagan's five minutes of free air time each week with five minutes from a representative of the opposition political party, the Democrats.

7. None. However, the Associated Press Radio Network did air a few minutes of the typically dull legislative session that day.

8. ABC split its radio network into four separate services: Information (aimed at news stations), Entertainment (aimed at middle-of-the-road stations), Contemporary (aimed at rock stations), and FM (aimed at classical music stations). This new system reflected the changing nature of radio, with more and more network affiliates now aiming for one particular segment of the audience ("narrowcasting"). As a result, ABC and the other networks found many programs being rejected by the affiliates because they did not fit into the local stations' specialized formats. To obtain more program clearances, ABC initiated its network split. So as not to violate the FCC's rule (from the 1940s) against the same network offering separate, competing services, ABC was careful to supply only one program from any of the four services in any given time slot. Technically, then, ABC was in compliance with the FCC rule.

9. NBC's youth-oriented radio network. Following the success of ABC in the mid-1970s with live-on-tape music specials aimed at young people, NBC began its own series. The first taped concert was a one-hour Willie Nelson show that played on February 9, 1979. On May 28, NBC expanded the concept (dubbed "the Source"), offering two minutes of youth-oriented news once an hour (six hours a day) along with more concerts and music specials. Twenty-one stations picked up the service. The schedule of feeds expanded to twenty-four hours a day on September 1, 1979.

10. Radioradio. CBS began Radioradio on April 26, 1982, and was the last of the four major networks to depart from the unitary program concept and diversify. Ironically, the name was the same as the title of a song ("Radio, Radio") by Elvis Costello, which blasted the complacency of radio broadcasting at the time.

11. Roger Ebert. Movie News was a one-minute capsule film review series that premiered on August 2, 1982. At the time, Ebert also

served as film critic for the Sun-Times, a Chicago newspaper, and
At the Movies, a syndicated television series. He had previously
been co-host of Public Television's Sneak Previews series.

12. *Julie Harris. Like its video parent, this radio version of the popular Public Television series was financed by Mobil Oil and distributed by WGBH in Boston. The radio version premiered on May 5,
1979.*

13. *National Educational Radio, a loosely organized network of
noncommercial radio stations.*

14. *RKO. On September 1, 1981, the company began offering two
separate overnight network services at the same time, via satellite.*

15. *The ABC Direction Network, with an adult-oriented format (beginning with fifty-seven affiliates), and the ABC Rock Network,
aimed at "album-oriented" rock radio stations (beginning with forty
affiliates). This brought the number of network program services offered by ABC up to six.*

16. *The Mutual Black Network. Mutual began the network on May
1, 1972, as part of a program to diversify its offerings to reach select
segments of the listening audience. In September 1979, Mutual sold
its controlling share in its black network to the Sheridan Broadcasting Corporation, which changed the network's name to the
Sheridan Broadcasting Network. A rival black network, the National Black Network, began operations on July 2, 1973.*

17. *By the U.S. Postal Service. The RKO radio network began operations on October 1, 1979, and did live three-minute newscasts
every half-hour for fourteen hours a day via land cable. However,
its longer feature programs were taped and sent through the mail.
In February 1980, RKO went to satellite distribution and expanded
to twenty-four-hour operations.*

18. *WCFL in Chicago. The network bought the station from the
Chicago Federation of Labor for $12.5 million in June 1979. Six
months later, Mutual also purchased WHN in New York from Storer
Broadcasting for $14 million.*

19. *A proposed ABC national music network, delivered by satellite, which was dropped just two weeks before its scheduled premiere on July 1, 1982.*

20. *KTSA in San Antonio. The station began its stereo broadcasting on July 23, 1982, the day the FCC approved the AM stereo system from Kahn Communication. KHJ in Los Angeles and KFRC in San Francisco joined the next day. In August 1982, the FCC also approved an AM stereo system from the Harris Corporation. WQXI in Atlanta was the first to use that stereo system, beginning on August 6, 1982.*

21. *Enterprise Radio. It went off the air on September 24, 1981.*

22. *Bob Keeshan, alias Captain Kangaroo. He began his five-minute features on January 21, 1980.*

23. *Larry Lujack and Tommy Edwards, two rock disc jockeys known affectionately on Animal Stories as Uncle Lar' and Li'l Tommy. The simple format of the show was reminiscent of the low-key humor series of the 1930s and 1940s: Lujack would read unusual but true stories about animals, and Edwards would react in wide-eyed amazement. Naturally, these bits also served as a springboard for banter that had absolutely nothing to do with animals. Though never syndicated or aired on the network, the program nonetheless developed a following across the country, especially in the Midwest, as a result of the wide coverage by WLS's AM signal and the successful distribution of two albums of excerpts from the show.*

24. *NBC claimed that it was the first live network radio drama in twenty-five years.*

25. *Mutual claimed it was the first live orchestra presentation on commercial network radio since 1954. The program was sent live to about fifty stations. The broadcast also marked the beginning of Mutual's multi-channel programming service, which offered subscribers up to seven different programming networks at the same time, via satellite.*

26. *Remote broadcasts of band concerts. In the 1930s, before recorded music was considered appropriate for radio, most networks and local stations filled much of their broadcast day with live pickups of bands performing at various locations. In the 1950s, with the cutbacks in network radio and the end of the big band era, most of these broadcasts ceased. CBS, however, kept supplying some band remotes to the dwindling number of stations that wanted such fare. By December 1971 only forty stations* in the country still aired CBS's Saturday morning band concerts, so the service was dropped.

27. *It marked the virtual end of the news-and-features approach to network programming that NBC had taken since the 1960s. The network axed almost all of its daily features and weekend public affairs shows, including* Man about Anything *with* Gene Shalit, Ask Dr. Brothers *with Joyce Brothers,* Willard's Weather *with Willard Scott,* Jensen Report *with Mike Jensen,* Here and Now *with Roger Mudd, and the long-running* Second Sunday. *Aside from hourly news, all that remained on the general NBC network were several two-minute* Comment on the News *features on weekdays and the Sunday audio rebroadcast of television's* Meet the Press.

FADE OUT/
SWITCH OFF

Fade Out/ Switch Off

1. What was the first network program to celebrate fifty years of regular broadcasting?

2. What was special about the date of Arthur Godfrey's final radio series broadcast for CBS: the April 30, 1972, edition of *Arthur Godfrey Time*?

3. When Don McNeill's *Breakfast Club* went off the air in 1968, how long had McNeill hosted the show?

4. On June 26, 1949, Jack Benny appeared as a special guest on the last regular radio program hosted by what veteran comic?

5. What eighty-four-year-old news commentator retired from CBS in 1976?

6. What weekly news documentary program usually closed with the tag line, "Time . . . marches on"?

7. How did each week's episode of *Dragnet* wrap up?

8. Did perennial adolescent Jack Armstrong ever reach adulthood?

9. On January 28, 1960, the BBC presented "The Last Smoking Seagoon," the final episode in the *Goon Show* series. Who wrote the script?

10. At the end of Orson Welles's unforgettable 1938 *Mercury Theater* version of "The War of the Worlds," how were the Martians defeated?

11. *The Hitch-Hiker's Guide to the Galaxy* revealed that an ancient alien race had discovered the answer to the ultimate question of life, the universe, and everything. What was it?

12. Who used this standard closing line: "Good night, Mrs. Calabash, wherever you are"?

13. With what standard exchange did Bob and Ray close their shows?

14. What was the last record played on WABC on May 10, 1982, before the station changed to all-talk programming?

15. Give the closing line of Paul Harvey's daily commentary program.

ANSWERS

1. Music and the Spoken Word. *This Sunday morning broadcast of the Mormon Tabernacle Choir from Salt Lake City premiered in July 1929 on NBC's Blue network. The show shifted to CBS in 1932, where it celebrated its fiftieth anniversary in 1979.*

2. *It marked twenty-seven years to the day of his first broadcast for the network on April 30, 1945. This also marked the end of the variety program format on the CBS radio network.*

3. *Thirty-five years and six months. McNeill started with the Pepper Pot program on the NBC Blue network on June 23, 1933, staying with the show as it changed its name to* The Breakfast Club. *That title remained even after the network itself changed from Blue to ABC. In the late 1960s, when ABC split into four networks,* The Breakfast Club *was renamed* The Don McNeill Show. *Under that title it ran briefly on the ABC Entertainment network until December 27, 1968, when the series at last ended.*

4. *Fred Allen, with whom Jack Benny had carried on a mock radio feud for years.*

5. *Lowell Thomas. He concluded forty-six years of network reporting on May 14, 1976. His* Lowell Thomas Reporting *had been on CBS since 1946.*

6. The March of Time.

7. *With a brief summary of the legal action taken against that week's criminals, detailing the charges, the sentences, and the actual punishment imposed.*

8. *Yes, in 1950. When the series title changed to* Jack Armstrong of the SBI *(Scientific Bureau of Investigation), the main characters—Jack, Billy, and Betty—became instant adults. This new show lasted only one season.*

9. *Spike Milligan. He wrote most of the scripts throughout the nearly ten-year run of the series in Britain.*

10. *They were destroyed by common Earth bacteria against which they had developed no built-up resistance.*

11. *"Forty-two." Unfortunately, none of them knew just what the precise question was, so the answer did not do them much good.*

12. *Jimmy Durante.*

13. *"This is Ray Goulding, reminding you to write if you get work. . . ." "And Bob Elliott reminding you to hang by your thumbs."*

14. *John Lennon's "Imagine." This was the last rock song played on what had been New York City's main rock outlet for almost twenty years before it went to an all-talk format.*

15. *"Paul Harvey . . . good day!"*